Learning About Sex

Love, Sex & God

A Guide for the Christian Family

For Discussion or Individual Use
Book 5 of the Learning about Sex Series for Boys

The titles in the series:

Book 1: Why Boys and Girls Are Different

Book 2: Where Do Babies Come From?

Book 3: How You Are Changing

Book 4: Sex and the New You

Book 5: Love, Sex, and God

Book 6: How to Talk Confidently with Your Child about Sex

Acknowledgments

We wish to thank all medical, child development, and family
life consultants who have assisted in the development, updating,
and revising of the Learning about Sex series.

Copyright © 1982, 1988, 1995, 1998, 2008, 2015
Concordia Publishing House
3558 S. Jefferson Ave., St. Louis, MO 63118-3968
1-800-325-3040 • www.cph.org

From text originally written by Bill Ameiss and Jane Graver
Unless otherwise noted all internal illustrations and photographs © iStock.com

Made in Dongguan, China / 055760 / 415080

4 5 6 7 8 9 10 11 12   27 26 25 24 23 22 21 20

CONTENTS

Editors' Foreword   4

Introduction   6

1.   Sex and Sexuality   8

2.   The Male and the Female Sexual Systems   18

3.   Sex and Your Health   34

4.   The Challenges of Becoming a Man   44

5.   Dating   64

6.   Finding Out If Love Is Real   88

7.   Marriage: When Two Become One   101

8.   When Two Become Three   109

Sexually Transmitted Disease (STDs)   124

Glossary   133

Foreword

This book is one of a series of six designed to help parents communicate Christian values to their children in the area of sexuality. *Love, Sex, and God* is the fifth book in the series. It is written especially for young men ages 14 and older and, of course, for the parents, teachers, and other significant adults who are concerned about their healthy development and may want to discuss the book with them.

Like its predecessor, the new Learning about Sex series provides information about the mental, emotional, physical, and spiritual aspects of human sexuality. Moreover, it does so from a distinctively Christian point of view, in the context of our relationship to the God who created us and redeemed us in Jesus Christ. The series presents sex as another good gift from God, designed by Him for us to share in marriage. It also may help us understand how God's design and gifts of sexuality and marriage fit in the larger context of our entire life of faith. To counter cultural influences, be strong and consistent in communicating the miracle of God's design. The way God made us is just the way He knew it should be for our health and happiness.

Each book in the series is graded—in vocabulary and in the amount of information it provides. It answers the questions that persons at each age level typically ask. Because children vary widely in their growth rates and interest levels, parents and other concerned adults will want to preview each book in the series, directing the child to the next graded book when he is ready for it.

Ideally, this book will be used as part of a biblically based, broadly focused—yet personal—training program to prepare young men for biblical manhood. For young men, this training can flow from a mentoring relationship similar to that of Paul and Timothy. A young man can learn much from a father, grandfather, or other Christian adult. In the context of such a relationship, questions of a personal nature can be asked and answered, insightful discussions held, and godly behaviors modeled.

Your expression of positive and God-pleasing values will likely have a greater impact on the healthy development of your son than any book, other than the Bible. God's plan unfolds as each generation in succession passes on the truths God imparts through His Word and the wisdom that comes as challenges are met and overcome by the power of God's grace through Jesus.

In addition to reading these books, parents can use them as starting points for casual conversation and when answering other questions children might have. We pray that this will be the beginning of ongoing open, honest, and intentional communication with your child regarding God's magnificent design.

The books in this series also can be used as mini units or as part of another course of study in a Christian school or church setting. Whenever the books are used in a class setting, it is important to let the parents know beforehand, since they have the primary responsibility for the sex education of their children. In a classroom setting, the books in this series are designed to be used with groups separated by their sex. This setting is most conducive to open conversation, encouraging questions that may be difficult to ask if members of the opposite sex are present. As the Christian home and the Christian school and church work together, God's design for marriage and sexuality can be more effectively taught.

It is important to communicate not only accurate information about the way God made us male or female, but especially a sense of wonder and deep appreciation of the beauty of God's marvelous design and purpose, and a sense of respect and responsibility toward all God has given.

The Editors

"Therefore a man shall leave his father and mother and hold fast to his wife, and the two shall become one flesh" (Ephesians 5:31).

Introduction

What does it mean to be made in the image and likeness of God?

What does it take to be a young man in today's culture?

What is God's design for sexuality anyway?

These are some pretty deep questions. Most people never pause to consider these matters. Even if you have, you probably still have some confusion. Sometimes the Bible seems so clear in its guidance for our lives, and other times it is pretty hard to understand. Making matters worse, the culture offers some pretty attractive and enticing lies about what sex is all about and what it means to be a young man in the world today.

As a young Christian man, you are in the midst of a great deal of change. Not only is your body continuing to mature, but your mental, emotional, and spiritual capacities are growing as well. You are growing more confident, strong, and wise, but you also may struggle with self-doubt, confusion about the world, and a growing sense that there must be more to faith in Jesus Christ than what you learned in Sunday School. Complicating everything is a growing sexual awareness that is both exciting and confusing. Just how are you supposed to put it all together?

The purpose of this book is to explore these and a whole range of related questions and subjects. We draw on the questions, struggles, and experiences of many young men who have grown to be strong Christian men. We'll try to help you use their questions and experiences together with reliable biological information as you work through what it means to be a Christian man who understands and honors God's design for marriage and sexuality.

The Bible reveals God's plan of salvation to us, the plan that sent Jesus Christ to save us from our sin. The Bible tells us that this forgiveness is ours in Christ. And the Bible describes what God's will is for Christian living as defined by the Ten Commandments. You are old enough now to know that no one can keep the Ten Commandments, but God still demands this of us. This is why we have the great news of forgiveness in Christ for our failure to live as God wills. For Christians, the Commandments also serve as a guide for godly living. Much of what we will discuss in this book revolves around the Sixth Commandment: "You shall not commit adultery." This commandment is further explained by the Rev. Martin Luther in his Small Catechism of the Christian faith. He states: "We should fear and love God so that we lead a sexually pure and decent life in what we say and do, and husband and wife love and honor each other" (Explanation of the Sixth Commandment). This commandment and explanation give us a wonderful description of God's design and will for marriage and sexuality in our lives. God strengthens us through the Holy Spirit to daily acknowledge our sin and to rejoice in the forgiveness Christ won for us. In thanksgiving to God for this, we respond with choices and behaviors that are according to His good will and that serve our neighbor. And for this discussion, your "neighbor" is your future wife.

Is it even possible to live according to God's standard for sexual purity?

What do I do with sexual temptation?

Sex and Sexuality

By God's Design Devotion

Read Ephesians 5:22–33.

"Therefore a man shall leave his father and mother and hold fast to his wife, and the two shall become one flesh" (Ephesians 5:31).

"What does God want?" You may ask this question when you are truly wondering about God's will for your life. At other times, you may shout in frustration and anger: "What does God *want* from me? Doesn't He get how hard it is to live up to His standard of sexual purity? Sex is everywhere! What does He expect?"

All young Christian men undergo this struggle. Do you feel that God has set up this standard just to see you fail? That isn't true. God isn't out to ruin your fun or make you miserable. God's high standard for sex is made just for our benefit. He designed sex to be *within marriage* and *very good*. He gives us marriage so we won't be lonely; He wants us to live a life filled with joy, companionship, and sexual pleasure. This is marriage by God's design.

Sin corrupted God's design for marriage. We have twisted sex and marriage almost beyond recognition—almost, but not quite. Christ loved His people, the Church, enough to die for us. What earthly parallel does God give us for that love? The love between a husband and wife. In marriage, you will recognize Christ's love for you too. May you be strengthened in Christ's love as you grow in Him.

Prayer: Jesus, I thank You for loving me and giving Your life to save me from death. Thank You for making men and women to love and care for each other. Give me patience and strength in these years as I discover who I am in You. Amen.

God's Plan for Sex and Our Sexuality

God made man and woman intentionally and in a very personal way. In the Book of Genesis (which means "in the beginning"), we read that we are set apart from the rest of creation. Unlike light, trees, birds, and other creatures, God didn't say, "Let there be . . . and there was." God designed us personally, and He designed us for each other.

In Genesis 1–2, the Bible tells us that on the sixth day, after everything else had been created by His Word, God then made man. He "formed the man of dust from the ground and breathed into his nostrils the breath of life, and the man became a living creature" (Genesis 2:7). When God made all the other creatures, He told them immediately to "be fruitful and multiply" (Genesis 1:22), so they were probably created in pairs that fit together. But at first there was only man, the male. God created everything else and saw that it was good, but He recognized that it was not good for man to be alone. Adam, too, needed a "helper fit for him" (Genesis 2:18). So God made a woman out of the man's rib and gave her to him, and him to her.

This is it! This is the crucial part of God's design for humans—He made them man and woman! The female was created for the male (that's you) so they would fit together into a complete whole. Man needs woman as much as woman needs man. Created for each other, Adam and Eve lived in harmony, in unity, and in close and perfect communication with each other and with God. God designed the perfect companion and helper for man—woman. They were given to each other by God; that is marriage, to be given to another for life!

God also said to them what He said to the rest of His creatures: "Be fruitful and multiply." That's where sexuality fits into the picture. Coming together sexually and having children is a beautiful part of God's design for the happiness and fulfillment of a husband and wife. God gave them sexual organs that fit together so that children could be born of man and woman. He gave them an intimacy in their relationship that is unique to marriage. The Bible calls this the "one flesh" union (Ephesians 5:31). When man and woman come together in marriage, they come together into one flesh. They are no longer two and cannot be separated.

Sex is the physical expression of this one-flesh union. In marriage, God gives emotional completeness, the opportunity to be helper and provider, and physical (sexual) pleasure. Adam and Eve, the first married man and woman, enjoyed an ideal existence in the Garden of Eden, an existence that received and rejoiced in God's gifts of sex and sexuality.

Sin Enters the Picture

But the complete happiness of our first parents did not last long. Satan tempted them, and rather than resisting, they sinned, placing themselves and all of creation into the devil's firm grasp. Still, God did not abandon those He had created in His image. He called out to Adam and then to Eve, asking them what they had done. Pronouncing punishment, God also included the promise of the Savior.

God identified the pain of childbirth as a consequence of Eve's sin; He also said that she would now resent her place under her husband's authority. He told Adam that the consequence for his sin would be pain and frustration in his physical work. He would also now be burdened with toil, sweat, and worry over his responsibility for Eve, for his children, and for the land and animals. All of this was—and remains—a consequence of human sin. Adam and Eve (and all of us who follow after them) would know disappointment, hardship, and heartache as results of the fall into sin. Sin would contaminate every aspect of their lives, including self-image, personal fulfillment and satisfaction, and relationships with both God and others. Sin now also corrupts our sexual desire and our ability to be faithful in all that we think, say, and do, and our marriages are now infected with selfishness.

God's people do not always follow His plan for their lives perfectly, but isn't it amazing that God receives us into His family in spite of our sin? He does this for Christ's sake, who died on the cross for our forgiveness. God desires that we obey Him—this is how we are to show our love for Him—but He is quick to forgive and restore us when we fall. This forgiveness and restoration is accomplished in and through Christ.

The Bible calls us to be transformed into the likeness of Christ (see 2 Corinthians 3:18). This is only possible when the Holy Spirit lives within us and daily works in us the process of sanctification, strengthening us for good works and holy living. When Paul writes about living holy lives, including sexual purity, he is not taunting us with some impossible task or trying to lay new burdens on us. He is actually describing the way things were by God's design in Genesis, in the beginning. And with our

Baptism into Christ, we are made a new creation and given a newness of life in Christ, where we have been freed to love Him and others as God designed.

This isn't to say it's easy, but all of life now requires daily recognition of our sin and daily receiving forgiveness from Christ. We live forgiven and now restored by the Holy Spirit, who enables us to live sexually pure lives. What we share together in this book is learning about who we are as Christian men—sinful but redeemed in Christ

This emphasis on sin, forgiveness, restoration and new life might seem out of place in a book about sexuality, but then again, maybe understanding these spiritual truths really *can* help us make our way through the challenges of life.

Is Being Male or Female Really That Important?

This may seem like a strange question, but some people really wonder if there is such a big difference. Our culture has been pushing the idea that masculinity and femininity are just social constructs—or, to put it another way, that our sex is created by society's attitudes and has no deeper meaning. In the 1960s and 1970s in America, many women took action to have more opportunities in a male-dominated society and to define new roles and identities. This feminist movement was also heavily influenced by the development of the **birth control** pill. Many women believed that control over when and if they got pregnant meant that they were now equally equipped to do whatever a man could do in the workplace and in matters of sexual activity. Unfortunately, this type of feminist attitude has now been pitting women against men for decades.

The Bible affirms that men and women have equal worth in God's eyes, but it is also clear that we are different by design. It's not just that males and females have different sexual organs—this much is obvious—but that our entire makeup is different. Research shows that men and women process information differently, have different physical strengths and weaknesses, and approach relationships differently. By God's design, male and female were created to *complete* each other, not to be exactly the same.

You began to be a male at the instant of your **conception**. Our sex is a biological fact. Our sex at the DNA level cannot be changed. It's an integral part of who we are as a person . . . who we were created to be.

During an ultrasound or at your birth, your parents joyfully said, "It's a boy!" From that moment on, everyone treated you as a boy. By age 2, you were watching other males very carefully so you could imitate their masculinity in walk, mannerisms, and speech. For as long as you live, you will experience life as a male. Your sex is central to who you are.

Rejoicing in our male and female differences isn't just a trendy social idea past its prime. For nearly all of human history, these differences have been recognized. They were sometimes celebrated and sometimes abused, but it was still okay for men and women to be different, to have different strengths and weaknesses. The sex blurring we see in culture today is a human twisting of God's good design.

Broken and Restored

Unfortunately, sin has negatively affected the way we understand ourselves as men, the way we relate to God, and our interactions with other men and women. All these relationships are broken by sin. The result is often physical or emotional pain because the way things are now is not God's original, perfect design for men and women.

We often act harshly toward others, even talking and acting disrespectfully to the men and women around us. We shake our fist at God because He won't condone what we are our doing when it gives us pleasure, even if we know it is wrong. We say it's okay and that we can do whatever makes us feel good. "God just doesn't want us to have fun!" we think.

We can cause hurt and discontent when we focus on how others should treat us instead of focusing on how we should treat others. And we have wounds deep inside of us—loneliness, guilt, anger, lust, sorrow—because we make choices that do not show a love for God and for the other people in our lives (our neighbors).

A way to describe the situation we are in is *broken*. We are broken people. We've been split apart and separated, so that we are no longer closely connected to God, to others, or to a right understanding of ourselves. Did you ever wonder why even a Christian as great as St. Paul struggled to do what he didn't want to do and didn't do what he wanted to do? (See Romans 7:14–25.) Sin has broken the harmony and unity between God and us, among us as men and women, and within us as our desires and behaviors often no longer reflect God's design.

But Jesus came to live, die, and rise again for all human sin. He came to break down the walls of hostility that separate us from God and from one another. He came to restore all that is broken in each of us—male and female. He came to create the "new self, which is being renewed in knowledge after the image of its creator" (Colossians 3:10), just like in the beginning.

In a very real sense, Jesus came to fix all that is broken. This is called reconciliation. He restores us to a loving relationship with God our Father. He brings forgiveness and grace to marriages and families. He even helps us overcome our selfish desires by the power and fruit of the Holy Spirit, who gives us love, joy, peace, patience, kindness, goodness, *faithfulness*, gentleness, and *self-control* (Galatians 5:22–23).

We are broken, but God restores! What a great and wonderful thing to be thankful for and to remember as a young Christian man!

The Deeper Meaning of Sex and Marriage

The big question for many Christians is not "Should I follow God's plan for sexual purity?" but "What does God's design for sex look like?" Another common question, especially for Christian young people, is "How far can I go without sinning?" Does this describe your attitude concerning sex? You want to follow God's plan for sexuality, but what exactly are the boundaries?

God's design outlines what your sexual behavior looks like before you are married and what your sexuality is within marriage. Knowing God's design and its importance will help you embrace it and defend it when challenged.

Marriage Is Important to God

Did you know that in the Bible, the story of God's people *begins* in Genesis with the marriage of a man and a woman (they are given to each other) and *ends* in the Book of Revelation with the marriage of the Lamb and the Bride at a great marriage banquet? This marriage between the Lamb and the Bride is also known as the marriage between Christ and all His believers (the Church).

What does this mean? God designed marriage to be a sign of Christ and His relationship with the Church. In fact, God uses marriage, faithfulness, infidelity, and forgiveness between husband and wife as themes throughout the Bible. Because God designed us as male and female, and because we know what marriage is, we get it when God uses "marriage words" to describe Christ and the Church. A husband sacrifices for his wife. Christ sacrificed His life for His people. We can understand this. A wife loves her husband deeply and desires to please Him. The Church submits to Christ, loving Him, thanking Him for His husbandly care, and looking to Him for all good things. We understand this! God uses everyday things so that we can better understand Him. Get it?

You will find marriage images throughout the Old Testament. God describes His relationship with His people in terms of a marriage. He calls Himself the Bridegroom, and Israel His Bride. He laments when Israel strays, just as a husband would weep over an unfaithful wife. One of His prophets, Hosea, is commanded to marry a **prostitute** as an illustration of how God loves us and is faithful to us, even though we are sinful and unfaithful to Him. Why? Because He *is* the faithful husband!

The marriage imagery continues in the New Testament. Not only did Jesus teach about marriage, He also used marital imagery when speaking to His followers. In Matthew 9:14–16, Jesus said His disciples did not fast because they were with the Bridegroom. By this, Jesus meant that when the Bride is with the Groom, it is a celebration! No fasting is allowed at a celebration. Fasting is like the depriving oneself of pleasure before the marriage feast. But the marriage feast is the giving of pleasure to each other! The boundary is clearly there: outside of marriage is sexual fasting; within marriage is feasting!

Later, St. Paul wrote about Jesus' work of *giving Himself up* for the Church in order to make her holy as a Bride for Himself. Again, marriage is the giving of self, not taking; and Christ is the perfect self-sacrificing Groom to His Bride (that's us)!

If you've ever attended a wedding, chances are you heard 1 Corinthians 13:4–8 read as part of the ceremony. In this chapter, Paul compares the love between a husband and a wife with the love Christ has for His Church. Read it for yourself:

"Love is patient and kind; love does not envy or boast; it is not arrogant or rude. It does not insist on its own way; it is not irritable or resentful; it does not rejoice at wrongdoing, but rejoices with the truth. Love bears all things, believes all things, hopes all things, endures all things. Love never ends" (1 Corinthians 13:4–8).

The passage from 1 Corinthians 13 is used at many weddings because it describes so beautifully what love within marriage looks like. But if you read these words through the eyes of a Christian, you will see the real message: Christ is love! He alone could give Himself up for us on the cross in perfect love to save us and make us holy. Your future marriage will strive to witness to Christ behind these words of love. When you are patient and kind, not selfish or resentful, when you support, encourage, and help your wife in her weaknesses, you are witnessing to the love that Christ first showed you and your future wife. What a joy to love in these terms! "We love because He first loved us" (1 John 4:19).

How Does Knowing about God's Design for Marriage Affect My Sexual Desires Now?

"Therefore a man shall leave his father and his mother and hold fast to his wife, and they shall become one flesh. And the man and his wife were both naked and were not ashamed" (Genesis 2:24–25).

The marriage of Adam and Eve from the beginning has everything to do with love, sex, and marriage for you today as a young Christian man. God designed us and set the boundary within marriage: "Man shall . . . hold fast to his wife, and they shall be come one flesh." We are still made according to God's original design, male and female, capable of becoming one flesh. And because He created us, God desires only what is best for us. He knows our weaknesses and promises to help us overcome the temptations and sin that are now a part of our lives and our world.

God's love for us can provide daily guidance as we strive to control our own sexual desires in a sinful world. God is love. His love for us is the best example we have of love.

This love was first was shown when He created male and female for each other. It is shown to us today through Jesus, who died for our sins on the cross so that we might be returned to God. God is love in that He created us and redeemed us in Jesus. And He is love in that He gives us the power through the Holy Spirit to live according to His design and will. Now we can show godly love to others.

If showing love to others, acting unselfishly, and following God's will regarding waiting until marriage to have sex seem difficult or even impossible at this point, remember that it is not our efforts that give us strength. It is Christ alone, living in us and working through us, that allows us to *daily* conform our desires to God's will. This will require understanding what it means to be a Christian man in a world often incompatible—even hostile—to the way God designed us to live. This will be difficult to hold on to when faced with the decisions your friends make about their sexuality. This will be a challenge that will require daily help. But your help comes by "looking to Jesus, the founder and perfecter of our faith, who for the joy that was set before Him endured the cross, despising the shame, and is seated at the right hand of the throne of God" (Hebrews 12:2). He is stronger than your desires and the ungodly opinions and attitudes of those around you. He is the Almighty One!

Practically speaking, the more you study God's Word, the more you will find strength to lead a sexually pure and decent life. Pray to God for strength also to resist temptation and to exercise self-control over your desires. They are strong, but God is stronger. And if your strength fails, remember His amazing love for you.

Part of growing into a mature, healthy man is learning to control all this amazing, creative, life-giving sexual energy and to channel it toward your future family. He created these desires within us to be strong so that they would work according to His design. Even with sin in our lives, God can strengthen and guide us on His path for our lives. Sexual desire is a good gift of God that allows us to bond to each other in ways that please Him. By valuing your sexual desire and reserving sexual expression for marriage, you are able to combat the cultural messages that work to cheapen sex. This is truly God-pleasing.

God loves us so much that He gave His only Son to be a sacrifice in our place! Despite humankind's fall into sin, God had mercy on us to make everything right between us—not because we deserved it, but because He loves us so much.

Let's think about it!

17

2

The Male and the Female Sexual Systems

By God's Design Devotion

Read Psalm 139:13–18.

"I praise You, for I am fearfully and wonderfully made. Wonderful are Your works; my soul knows it very well" (Psalm 139:14).

Look in the mirror. What do you see? Do your eyes fall first on what you like about yourself or on what you don't like? Often, when we look in the mirror, we just see our "flaws," the places we think are too big or too small, too greasy or too flaky. And it's easy to think that everyone else looks at those things too.

While looking in the mirror, you may lose sight of the opinion that matters most. God looks at you and says, "I made you how you are. I personally knit you together before you were born. You are just the right size and shape, because I created you to be that way. I loved you so much that I sent Jesus to defeat death on the cross and restore our relationship. Because you are washed in His blood, I don't even see your sin. You are perfect to Me. I will always love the person you are."

> **Prayer: God, Your thoughts are so precious to me. I treasure every word You speak to me. Sometimes I forget how amazing You are and how much You love me. Help me to always remember who I am in Your eyes. In Jesus' name. Amen.**

One of the most remarkable examples of how wonderfully and intricately we were made occurs right in our own bodies. Have you ever paused to wonder at the design of your own body? God made you according to His design, and you are extraordinary!

Maybe you have felt uncomfortable with yourself, especially as you begin **puberty** and **adolescence**. This is natural because you are going through a lot of changes physically, emotionally, and intellectually. You are also experiencing spiritual growth as you seek to better know and understand Christ and all He has done for you. As a teenager, you may be very self-conscious about your voice changing, growing facial hair, or having these changes occur earlier or later than your friends. The truth is that almost every young person feels uncomfortable with himself or herself at some point.

However, there is a danger if you allow your discomfort to become a kind of hatred or even a disappointment with your body. We know our bodies aren't perfect because of the effects of sin, but we also know that God was directly involved in our creation. He made *you* how you are today!

Do you blame God for what you look like—a big nose or skinny arms, whether you are tall or short, heavy or thin? Did God make a mistake with you? It might be tempting to think so, but God knew what He was doing, and He loves you as you are.

It is tempting to just look at the outside of a person and think he is really strong or she is really cute, but beneath the surface, we are all "fearfully and wonderfully made" (Psalm 139:14). Don't think so? Consider your eyes, which allow you to read this book, or your brain, which helps you translate the words on this page into meaning. What about the breath you just took? You didn't even have to think about it, yet it happened. When you take time to look at all the amazing systems in your body, you can see that your body is truly awesome by God's design.

This is no less true for your reproductive system and sexual organs. You may not even think much about this part of your body yet, but it is just as amazingly designed by God.

The Male Sexual System

"For from Him and through Him and to Him are all things" (Romans 11:36).

God designed a man's body to be special and different from a woman's body. He has given you the organs to deliver **sperm** to fertilize your wife's egg cell so that a baby might be nurtured in her **uterus**. God has given you the sexual organs so that you will enjoy giving and receiving pleasure during **intercourse** with your wife. God's design for you and how you will fit with a future wife is "very good."

The Male Reproductive Organs

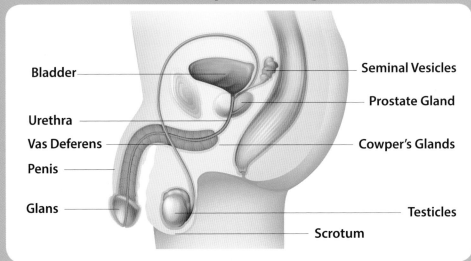

Bladder

Urethra

Vas Deferens

Penis

Glans

Seminal Vesicles

Prostate Gland

Cowper's Glands

Testicles

Scrotum

The Testicles

The **testicles** are roundish glands that hang just behind the **penis** in a pouch called the **scrotum**. Why is the left testicle lower (and sometimes larger) than the right one? Is this a mistake in God's creation? No—it's really a miracle of design, for it keeps the testicles from getting hurt as the legs come together.

Consider, too, God's wisdom in putting the testicles in the scrotum— outside the rest of the body. In this way the testicles are able to maintain the temperature they need—about 4 degrees lower than the rest of the body. In cold weather, the muscles of the scrotum contract to bring the testicles close to the body. In warm weather, the muscles relax to lower the testicles away from the body. In this way the testicles are always kept near the proper temperature.

A boy's testicles are inside his body until a few weeks before he is born. Then the testicles descend into the scrotum. As a boy matures into a young man, the testicles produce sperm, tiny cells that are needed for reproduction. From puberty into old age, these amazing glands make millions of sperm a day. Sperm can be seen only through a microscope; one drop of seminal fluid can contain 120 million of them. They look like tadpoles with skinny, active tails.

Another important job of the testicles is to produce **testosterone**, a

hormone or chemical that controls the development of male sex characteristics—like a beard and lower voice. During puberty, boys notice that the testicles and penis grow and become darker in color; hair grows in the **pubic** area and later on the body and face; the voice deepens; muscles and bones grow very rapidly. For young men as well as for young women, interest in the opposite sex begins to emerge, preparing them for adulthood and marriage.

The Sperm Storage and Transportation System

After sperm are produced in tiny tubes inside the testicles, they move to larger tubes, where they mature. Then they travel through another tube (the **vas deferens**) to the **seminal vesicles**, which are two pouches just behind the **bladder**. Next to the seminal vesicles is an active little gland, the **prostate**. It constantly manufactures a fluid that mixes with fluids from other glands to make **semen**. Semen is the white, sticky fluid in which sperm leave the penis. Only 1–3 teaspoons of semen leave the body at any one time.

The Penis

The penis hangs in front of the testicles. Like the testicles, the penis is very sensitive to contact. The **glans**, the end of the penis, is especially sensitive. It is covered with a loose elastic skin, the **foreskin**.

Many doctors recommend **circumcision** (removing the foreskin) to prevent dirt or urine from collecting under the foreskin and thus causing infection. Usually this simple operation is done soon after birth, but it can be done at any age. Circumcision does not affect a male's ability to give or receive sexual pleasure. Some parents choose not to have this procedure performed. With or without the foreskin, the penis functions the same way.

© iStock.com / Clinton Johnston

Erections

When a man is sexually aroused, the soft, limp tissue of his penis becomes erect and larger—hard enough to stand away from the body. Even though there is a difference in the size and shape of penises, there is little difference in the sexual satisfaction for either man or woman.

The inside of a penis is a lot like a sponge. During an **erection**, extra blood rushes into the penis. Valves close to hold this blood under pressure.

Erections can happen at any age, but they begin to happen more frequently during adolescence. Even as it is a challenge for a girl to learn how to manage her period, an erection can happen to you unexpectedly and can be a challenge for you to control. An erection can be caused by sexual feelings and daydreams, but it can also occur because of tight clothing, pressure from a full bladder, or even for no apparent reason. Although it can be very embarrassing when it happens in public, it is usually not very noticeable to other people. One of the first types of sexual self-control an adolescent boy learns is how to better control these unexpected erections.

Ejaculation

If the stimulation that causes an erection is continued, semen moves into the **urethra** tube. Strong muscles move it along until it squirts or oozes from the penis. This **ejaculation** of semen brings feelings of pleasure, called an **orgasm**. Although semen and urine both leave the body through the urethra, they cannot pass through the penis at the same time. Special muscles close off the bladder when the penis is erect.

When the seminal vesicles are full, ejaculation may take place during sleep. This is called a **nocturnal emission** (or "**wet dream**"). While your body sleeps, your mind may experience stimulating dreams that cause sexual arousal. The increased hormone levels in your body can cause this spontaneous ejaculation.

Sometimes young men feel guilt or embarrassment about nocturnal emissions, but they are completely natural. They are part of God's design for how your body matures and gets ready to become a husband and a father.

These intricate parts of a man's body each have a purpose that fulfills

God's design, but femaleness also fits His creative design. Because you are a man, you will fit a woman and may be able to have children. You will be able to enjoy sexual intimacy with your future wife because you have the unique parts of a man.

The Female Sexual System

"For from Him and through Him and to Him are all things" (Romans 11:36).

God designed a woman's body to be special and different from a man's body. He has given a woman the organs to protect and nurture a baby in her uterus. God has given your future wife the sexual organs that enjoy giving and receiving pleasure during intercourse with you. God's design for your future wife and how she fits with you is "very good."

The Internal Sexual Organs

A sign of God's wonderful design is the difference between male and female sexual organs. Whereas most of the male reproductive system is outside the body, most of the female reproductive system is inside the body.

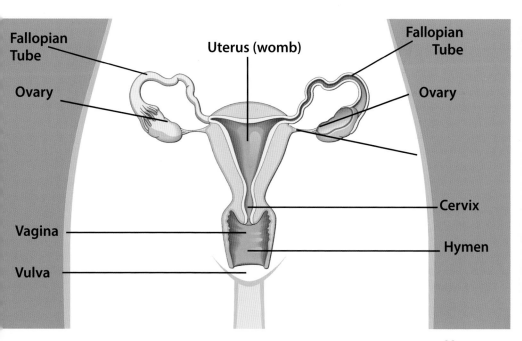

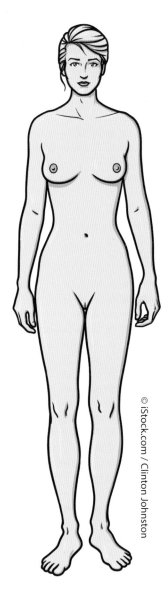

© iStock.com / Clinton Johnston

Deep inside the female body are a pair of **ovaries**. They contain thousands of undeveloped egg cells. When a girl is somewhere between the ages of 9 and 16, her ovaries begin to produce **estrogen**, the female hormone that controls many changes in her body.

During the next few years, her breasts develop and her hips broaden. Her height and weight increase rapidly. And her **sex organs** grow.

Hair appears under her arms and in her pubic area. As **menstruation** begins, she may also notice a clear, whitish discharge from her **vagina**. This is a way for the body to regulate and clean the vagina—another example of God's amazing design!

At puberty, the egg cells in the ovaries begin to ripen. About once every 28 days, a ripe egg cell bursts out of the **follicle** that has nourished it and leaves the ovary. The ripe egg is swept into the nearby **fallopian tube** by fluids and tiny hair-like **cilia** on the inside of the tube. **Fertilization**, the uniting of a mature egg cell with a sperm cell, when it happens, almost always happens in the fallopian tube.

Immediately, the covering of the egg cell changes to block the entry of other sperm. The new cell that has been created moves slowly into the uterus.

In a mature woman, the uterus is about the size and shape of a large pear. The walls of the uterus are made of extremely elastic muscles, able to stretch enough to hold a baby during **pregnancy**. These same powerful muscles contract downward to make childbirth possible. They also contract during menstruation, sometimes causing cramps in some women.

The vagina, or birth passageway, is a tube also made of elastic muscle. The walls of the vagina touch each other most of the time, much like a collapsed balloon. During sexual excitement, the vagina expands and produces a lubricating fluid that makes intercourse easier.

The **cervix**, or neck of the uterus, which opens into the vagina, is made of muscles that close tightly during pregnancy but stretch enormously during childbirth. No human engineer could design such a perfect system for beginning and supporting a new life! It's another miracle by God, the Master Designer!

The Vulva, or External Sexual Organs

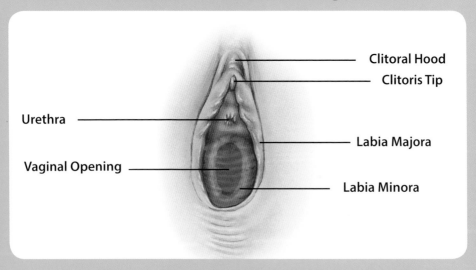

The opening of the vagina is partly covered by the **hymen**, a membrane that may be broken the first time **sexual intercourse** occurs. At one time, an unbroken hymen was important proof that a girl had not had sex and was a **virgin**. We now know that it often is broken much earlier in life without the girl realizing it. It is not a sign or mark of a woman's virginity.

Surrounding the opening to the vagina are two folds of skin, the labia majora (major lips). The outer sides are covered with hair. They serve as protection for the genital area.

Inside these are two more folds of skin, the labia minora (minor lips). Sometimes they are hidden by the major lips; sometimes they stick out between them. They may be pink or brown, wrinkled or smooth.

At the top of the labia minora is a small cylinder of very sensitive tissue, the **clitoris**. A woman may be able to see the pea-sized end of it with a mirror, or it may be hidden by the folds of the labia.

Between the clitoris and the vagina is the **urethra**, where urine leaves the body. It is very small and is completely separate from the vagina.

Menstruation

Most girls will start to menstruate ("have a period") as they grow into womanhood. You've probably heard things about a woman's period that are true and things that are not true, or myths.

Which of the following common myths have you heard?

- ☐ Menstruation is dirty because blood is leaving the body.
- ☐ A menstruating woman should avoid exercise, especially swimming.
- ☐ Menstrual cramps are not real.
- ☐ Women cannot handle demanding jobs because their menstrual cycle produces mood changes and uneven levels of energy.

The preceding statements are all false. But these myths have been widely believed for so many years that nearly everyone is affected by the attitudes they represent. Because there is a kernel of truth in each of them, you need detailed, factual information about menstruation to separate the truth from the myth.

UNCOVER THE FACTS

HERE IT IS:

It's Dirty

Myth 1: Menstruation is dirty because bad blood is leaving the body.

The Facts: The menstrual flow is a mixture of blood and cell fragments. When a ripe cell leaves the ovary, the uterus prepares for the possible beginning of a new life. Hormones (estrogen and **progesterone**) cause a soft, thick lining to form on the uterus walls. Extra blood flows to the uterus, ready to nourish a fertilized egg.

When fertilization does not happen, the egg cell, the new lining, and the extra blood are not needed. They break up and flow out through the vagina. This process happens about once a month for 25–40 years. Since God makes every person unique, the menstrual cycle is a little different for each woman.

Although menstruation is a normal, healthy process, some girls are embarrassed by it, especially in the early years. This feeling usually goes away when they become more used to their monthly cycles and learn how best to manage their period.

Perhaps the "dirty" label began because in very ancient times it was taught that during her period a woman was "unclean," not in a dirty sense, but in a "not touchable" sense. It was thought to be inappropriate to have sexual intercourse with her during her period. And today, most married people still choose to not have sex during a woman's period—not because it is dirty, but because it can be messy.

It is not true that a woman is unclean or dirty while having her period. However, as a young Christian man, it is important that you not make fun or tease young women about their periods. A girl maturing into a woman is a thing to be celebrated. Their bodies are preparing to hold a new life, a blessing from God. By appreciating this wonderful design now, you will be better equipped to help and support your future wife as she monthly deals with her period.

It's an Illness

Myth 2:   A menstruating woman should avoid exercise, especially swimming.

The Facts: Menstruation is a sign of a healthy, normal body.

Although many women have times when they feel uncomfortable during their periods, they can and should carry on normal activities. Most women feel best if they exercise moderately rather than strenuously.

Following ordinary healthy habits is especially important at this time: a woman should get enough rest, drink plenty of fluids, and avoid salt to prevent fluid retention.

It's Imaginary

Myth 3:   Menstrual cramps are not real.

The Facts: Menstrual pain is real; 90–95 percent of all women of reproductive age have physical symptoms during their period. For some women, hormonal changes just before menstruation produce a variety of symptoms called premenstrual syndrome (PMS). The most common are cramps, aching muscles and joints, low back pain, a feeling of fullness (bloating), fatigue, constipation or diarrhea, changes in sleep patterns, and breast tenderness. Besides these physical symptoms, women may also experience anxiety, irritability, or mood swings.

There are ways women can reduce the severity of PMS. Women who notice PMS symptoms should cut down on salt, sugar, and caffeine during the week before menstruation. Studies show that daily exercise will give relief to women who suffer from menstrual pain. Foods rich in thiamine and riboflavin (such as eggs, dairy products, and whole-grain products) may help fight PMS. Decreasing a woman's level of stress also helps.

It Affects Job Performance

Myth 4:   Women cannot handle demanding jobs because their menstrual cycle produces mood changes and uneven levels of energy.

The Facts: Other symptoms of PMS besides physical ones may include anxiety, irritability, tension, depression, mood swings, or fatigue. Many women feel especially energetic or exceptionally happy midway between periods, when a mature egg leaves the ovary. The extra hormones produced at that time can boost her energy level and make her feel good all over.

Two weeks later, her hormone level drops—just before she begins to menstruate. She may feel tired and sad. It is not kind to make fun of a woman as she experiences changing emotions. Everyone experiences mood swings, feeling tired, and sadness. Stress, worry, confusion, and uncertainty can all cause these emotional changes in both men and women. We all need to learn about ourselves and adjust to these changes.

Everyone can benefit from a healthy diet and regular exercise. Regular Bible study and devotional time can have an amazing effect on a person's outlook. A Christian man or woman can be thankful for all of God's blessings and be strengthened by the Spirit to find joy in Christ's love for us and the work He has given us to do each day. That is a great feeling!

Common Questions

Sometimes it is good to learn from the questions that young men like you have asked, questions like the ones that follow. You can read the answers for yourself, or even better, you might talk to your dad or another older man you trust. This might be awkward at first, but their wisdom and experience will be very helpful as you strive to understand all that you are experiencing right now.

The other boys make fun of me because I have so much fat on my chest that it looks like I have breasts. What is wrong with me?

There is probably nothing wrong with you. Chest enlargement is very common among adolescent boys due to the changes in hormone levels in a young man's body. It is a temporary condition and has no connection with your masculinity.

Is it okay to masturbate?

Masturbation occurs among both males and females because of the pleasurable feeling it produces. Touching the penis or the clitoris or **vulva** can create such feelings and can lead to the release of sexual pressure. This is called an orgasm. When a person touches himself to produce those feelings of pleasure, it is called self-stimulation, or masturbation.

Some people maintain there is nothing wrong with masturbating, and others think it is harmful or sinful. So, what is true?

First, let's go back to God's design in the beginning. God designed sex to be pleasurable for the man and the woman, but He designed this pleasure to be shared with the person "fit" for them. This would be the person given to you in marriage. In marriage, all of the pleasures of sexual stimulation and pleasure are guilt-free, an expression of love, and a some-times overwhelming desire to be joined. Remember the one-flesh nature of marriage that the Bible speaks about?

Also consider this: when a person masturbates, he or she usually also thinks sexual thoughts about another person or maybe recalls sexual images stored in the brain from sexually graphic movies or shows, video games, or even explicit **pornography**. While the Bible doesn't specifically speak about masturbation, it does strongly condemn lusting after others. Jesus went so far as to say that lusting after another person is the same as committing **adultery** (Matthew 5:28). Masturbation certainly strays away from the meaning of the commandment that says we are to live sexually pure and decent lives in what we say and do.

Some might say that they are able to masturbate without looking at pornography or lusting. Is it wrong then? Well, consider again God's good design. He made males and females to complement each other, and He de-signed their sexual organs to work together to give pleasure to their spouse and to produce new life. Nowhere in the Bible does God instruct us to live for ourselves. This holds true for our sexuality as well. Masturbation is an act for self-pleasure, requiring no one else, and thereby strays from God's design for sexuality.

Another concern about masturbation is that it can easily become habit forming. If masturbation becomes a habit, then a person is actual-ly conditioning himself or herself to receive sexual pleasure apart from another person.

Medically speaking, it is not harmful unless it becomes self-abusive. Medical authorities agree that aside from frequent or rough masturbation causing minor skin irritation, there are not really any harmful physical effects caused by masturbation. And the culture that surrounds us today usually makes light of masturbating, giving it the "wink-wink" that implies everyone is doing it and that it is okay. Consider how the release of these powerful neurochemicals makes stopping masturbation difficult. The good feeling created by the neurochemicals offers an opportunity for a person to get a quick emotional boost. It can easily become a compulsion or a psychological addiction! It may start to occupy your thoughts and interfere with your daily activities/schedule. Masturbation is not God's design for our use of the gift of sex because God intended that our sexual activity be shared with a spouse in mutual love and within the commitment of marriage.

It seems like everyone masturbates. How can I not?

If masturbation is a temptation for you, or if you have given in to this temptation, recognize the guilt that you feel as an understanding of God's good design for sex and your failure to honor God with your body. Turn immediately to Jesus and ask for forgiveness, which He freely gives to all and for all sins. Ask also for the power to resist and overcome this temptation. Focus on God's good design and the awesome joy that awaits you in marriage. Be strong in the Lord!

Learning to control your sexual desires is not easy, but a good word to help you is also an old word that has fallen out of favor in modern society: **chastity**. This word means to keep oneself pure and to order our sexual desires rightly. A chaste person understands the godly meaning and purpose of sexuality and strives to bring his desires in line with that truth. Chastity is a lifelong commitment. Unlike **abstinence**, chastity doesn't end once you get married. Just because you have a wife doesn't mean you can then become sexually impure. You will still need to approach your wife with pure motives and work for her good, rather than using her merely for your own needs.

One of the greatest and deepest joys you may have will be the pure, intense, and self-giving love you can share with your wife. This may not occur if you practice self-serving love as a young man.

Here are some ways to overcome the temptation or the habit of masturbation: Spend more time in activities with others, such as sports, clubs, hobbies—whatever interests you and will bring you into contact with people. Exercise also releases endorphins that boost your mood. By sharing God's love through acts of service and volunteerism, you will find a sense of satisfaction and love. Avoid pictures and books and conversations that are sexually stimulating. "Whatever is true, . . . whatever is pure, whatever is lovely, . . . think about these things," writes the apostle Paul (Philippians 4:8). In other words, think about all the exciting, interesting, beautiful things and people in God's world.

Most of all, ask God for His strength and power to resist temptation. "No temptation has overtaken you that is not common to man. God is faithful, and He will not let you be tempted beyond your ability, but with the temptation He will also provide the way of escape, that you may be able to endure it" (1 Corinthians 10:13–14).

What happens when a woman's vagina is too small for a man's penis?

This is not a problem you will face. The walls of the vagina are elastic enough to permit the birth of a baby; an erect penis is much smaller. When a woman is sexually aroused, her vagina gets bigger and produces a fluid that lubricates the inner walls to make receiving the penis pleasurable.

I'm shorter than the other guys, and my sex organs haven't developed much. Is there something wrong with me?

Physical changes are triggered by each person's individual time clock. Because of this, some fourteen-year-olds look like adults while others, equally normal, still look like young boys. And it's okay, even after you're done growing, if you're still shorter than many other men.

Your sex organs will grow and develop according to your biological clock also. Whatever insecurity you may feel about the size of your sex organs, remember that all of us are different. Your ability to give and receive pleasure with your future wife does not have anything to do with the size of your sex organs. There is no need to compare yourself with others. You are uniquely made male, with all the correct parts that make you that way.

Why do so many people think
the sexual parts of our bodies are dirty?

Many people haven't stopped to think about how precisely, how wonderfully, each of us is made. God designed our bodies intentionally and personally. He made them uniquely male and female, with all the parts that will bring completeness in marriage. The first married couple, Adam and Eve, were able to be completely naked and unashamed with each other. But when sin entered the world, so did shame, guilt, and a fear of being vulnerable. Ever since then, humans have felt differently about their bodies and have had more difficulty seeing them as the gifts of God they really are.

Our culture really impacts our perceptions of our own bodies and sexuality. Even though the culture seems to worship sex, it really debases it by making it common, an animal instinct or drive, or a tool to be used to get something else that is wanted. Women are often portrayed as sexually permissive and as objects for men's sexual desires. This degrades everyone's views of women. Men often believe that masculinity requires sleeping with many women and being able to have sex for hours at a time. This diminishes men and holds them to a very low standard of sexual behavior. In fact, it almost equates them with animals, who can't control their instincts to mate.

Men and women can *and do* exercise self-control, from adolescence through old age. For some, such self-control is just a matter of principle or sound health. For Christian men and women, it is primarily a desire to live sexually pure and decent lives out of thanksgiving to God for making us His children. Living by God's design has the added benefit of being a morally right and physically healthier lifestyle.

Sadly, sometimes well-meaning Christians give the impression that sex is dirty by refusing to talk about it in appropriate ways with their children. The parents likely are just uncomfortable talking about sex, which can inadvertently give the impression that sex is something that needs to remain secret and filled with shame.

Chapter 4 will discuss some of the other ways the culture lies about sex, and it will encourage you to cling to a godly understanding.

Sex and Your Health

By God's Design Devotion

Read Hebrews 4:14–16.

"Let us then with confidence draw near to the throne of grace, that we may receive mercy and find grace to help in time of need" (Hebrews 4:16).

Are you hearing things like this?

- ☐ **Doing drugs isn't bad for you; they just help you relax.**

- ☐ **Drinking at a party isn't a big deal.**

- ☐ **How are you still a virgin? Everyone else is having sex.**

- ☐ **Do you think you're better than us?**

It's easy to convince yourself that joining in with drugs, drinking, and sex is okay. You want to fit in. You justify your words and actions in your mind because you want people to like you; we all do! Deep down, though, you know these things are wrong. You haven't forgotten that. It's just easier to forget about it right now. There's a lot of pressure in your life! If everyone else you know is doing these things, are they really wrong? The temptation to just give in is huge.

Jesus gets it! Jesus understands your weakness because He was tempted in every way that you are. He is truly a man. But He is also truly God, and He resisted that temptation for you! Because He was sinless, He died on the cross as the perfect sacrifice for you. He did this so that you can be forgiven when you sin. Does that mean it is okay to give up and give in? No. But it does mean that you can ask Him to help you. He understands how hard it is. You can have confidence to approach Him and ask for help. He will give you grace to help in time of need. He has been there, and He has overcome all temptation for you.

> **Prayer: Dear Jesus, thank You for coming to earth to live a sinless life for me. Please forgive me when I sin and give me the strength to resist temptation every day. Remind me of Your mercy and grace. Amen.**

Despite God's glorious design for sex and marriage, many people think they can sidestep this plan and suffer no consequences. Why wouldn't they? Many of the messages in our culture encourage people to do what feels good, to serve themselves, and to have fun no matter what. But this is not what God created us for.

Confusion about God's plan for our lives trickles down into confusion about our sexuality. Have you ever heard anyone say (or thought yourself) any of the following statements?

YES/NO

☐ ☐ I need to have sex before I'm married to get experience. What if I get married and can't do it right?

☐ ☐ I'm too fat for anyone to love me.

☐ ☐ Drinking a little alcohol will make me more fun and interesting.

☐ ☐ Nice people don't get STDs.

☐ ☐ Oral sex and anal sex aren't really sex.

☐ ☐ Living together outside of marriage isn't really all that bad, right? Plenty of people seem to be doing it.

☐ ☐ If you lose your virginity, it can be restored.

All of these statements are myths; none of them is correct. But these myths are so common that we all need up-to-date information about each of them.

Inexperience

Myth 1: I need to have sex before I'm married to get experience. What if I get married and can't do it right?

The Facts: Some young people may worry that not having experience with sex before they are married will make sex in marriage awkward or not as good. This is simply not true!

People do learn how to have intercourse through practice—but two inexperienced married people can learn together without shame, guilt, or fearing their own awkwardness or inexperience. Their sexual intimacy will improve with practice—considerate, mutually satisfying practice. Such close intimacy within the safety of a marriage commitment allows both parties to trust that they have all the time in the world to figure out each other's needs and wants. This is impossible to do outside the security of marriage.

In marriage, there is a comfortable trust that even if first attempts at sex aren't the most amazing sexual experiences, it won't affect or end the relationship. In marriage, there is a level of care and concern for the other person's experience that is unequaled by the more temporary, self-serving sex outside of marriage. The love expressed, the patience husbands and wives share with each other, and the desire to please each other are characteristics of sex within marriage.

Deeply satisfying sexual relationships are far more than just physical unions. They involve rich emotional, mental, and spiritual bonds between two people who have pledged to give themselves in love to each other. Such bonds cannot *truly* or *completely* form outside of marriage because God does not bless nonmarried unions.

Imagine this scenario of a young man speaking to his girlfriend: "I think I love you and would like to have sex with you for a while, but I make no guarantees or promises that I will love you enough to marry you, and I can't vow to remain with you for the rest of our lives. But we can learn a lot about sex."

If a young man were that honest with a young woman, what do you think she'd do? Most of us would never be that crass, but if we try to experience sexual activity outside of marriage, that's precisely what we are saying. We're admitting that our sexual partner is probably not the person we'll be promising to spend the rest of our life with, but we want to use her to "practice" until the right person comes along.

Through Christ, we are new creations. If you are currently involved in a sexual relationship, know that you are forgiven through Jesus. All sinners come to Christ to repent and receive forgiveness. And in thanksgiving for our forgiven status, and with the power of the Holy Spirit, we now strive to live sexually pure and decent lives, honoring God with our bodies.

Weight Issues

Myth 2: I'm too fat for anyone to love me.

The Facts: To be lovable, a person first needs to be loved by God. And you are loved by God. He personally knit you together, died to redeem you, and gave you faith in Him.

Because God loves you, you are able to love others (1 John 4:19). God daily enables you to be a loving person because He pours out His limitless, unconditional love for you—which He reveals in His Word, the Bible. In joy and confidence, serve your family and your friends with kind acts, thoughtful words, and encouragement. Someday you may have the chance to serve your wife in this way, who will love, comfort, help, lead, and, yes, desire you. For now, pray to God for patience, for confidence in yourself, and for opportunities to serve and love the people around you. Sharing God's love with others will bless you at the same time!

Reaching out to your parents is often a big help if you are trying to understand what makes you lovable. Your family loves you and wants to support you in your efforts to be the most physically, emotionally, and spiritually healthy person you can be. Your parents were the first people to accept you just as God made you. Trust their words of advice and comfort as you learn that you are made by God's design to serve others in your life. Right now you may be a son, brother, and friend to others. Someday you may be a boyfriend or husband. Allow God's plan to unfold for you without worry or concern. Love yourself because God loves you. It can be that simple.

Let's think about it!

Myth 3:   Drinking a little alcohol will make me more fun and interesting.

The Facts: Establishing a happy physical and emotional relationship with another person is not easy. It's not surprising that people are willing to believe that alcohol or drugs will help make relationships easier. But medical evidence shows that alcohol is not a stimulant; it is a depressant. Why does a man imagine he is more mature by drinking alcohol? Drinking proves nothing about someone's maturity.

In fact, alcohol might make you act immaturely. Alcohol works first on the brain area that controls judgment and thought. The alcohol may make you feel more relaxed, but it will also make your thinking fuzzier and diminish your ability to make good decisions.

Nor is it good to encourage a young woman to drink. If you want to trap a girl into making a choice she would not make while thinking clearly, you are not acting in her best interest. Rather, you are serving yourself. Do you really want to begin a new relationship of any kind knowing her decision to be with you was influenced by alcohol?

Drinking too much alcohol can make a man temporarily **impotent** (unable to perform sexual intercourse, usually because erection of the penis cannot be achieved or sustained). The problem usually disappears when the alcohol leaves his system. However, if impotence is related to a longtime habit of drinking, the problem may be a permanent one.

God's Word reminds Christians that we don't need to get drunk. We have a better alternative: "Do not get drunk with wine, for that is debauchery, but be filled with the Spirit" (Ephesians 5:18).

Many people incorrectly believe that marijuana is a sexual stimulant. What it really does is distort a person's picture of reality. Using marijuana, or any illegal drug, creates artificial feelings that can fool you into believing things about yourself, others, and the world around you that simply aren't true. Drugs don't make you happier. They don't make you a more interesting person. And by using them, you abuse your mind and body.

Evidence from one study suggests that male marijuana smokers are more likely to be impotent than nonusers. Another study found a definite link between heavy marijuana smoking and reduced levels of sperm and of the male hormone testosterone.

Read the Ephesians 5:18 text again: "Do not get drunk . . . , but be filled with the Spirit." This is a good text to remember when you're faced with the temptation to use marijuana or any other harmful drug. If you are tempted to try drugs or alcohol, carefully consider the following question: is your life devoted to God or to yourself? Using marijuana only serves self, often at the expense of others. Alcohol use is often the same. Engaging in activities that may tempt us to sin takes us farther away from God.

Often, the use of drugs or alcohol masks a problem that you are trying to avoid dealing with. Whether it is uncertainty about yourself, others, or God, or conflict within your family, you may want to talk to a parent, pastor, or even a Christian counselor to help you sort out the problem or conflict. Drugs or alcohol seem like a fix at first because they mask some of the pain, even if only for a little while. But any substance or behavior that is used to dull pain or avoid dealing with a problem will eventually begin to control you. This is the basis for many addictions.

The mark of a Christian man is his faith demonstrated by service to God and to others. Sometimes this means getting help that you need from others to guide you through difficult times. Christians talking and working together will help you make decisions and choose behaviors that honor God and His design for your body. It may also help you find the meaningful relationships you desire.

Sexually Transmitted Diseases

Myth 4:   Nice people don't get STDs.

The Facts: Sexually transmitted diseases (STDs) are diseases that are usually passed from person to person by close sexual contact. They have nothing to do with whether you are "nice" or not! If you engage in sexual activity before marriage, especially with multiple partners, you greatly increase your risk of getting an STD. The only way to prevent STDs is to have sex with just one person—your wife. Pray that she has also honored God's design for her body by remaining a virgin until she is married. Of course, once you are married, you and your wife will remain faithful to each other and in this way continue to prevent getting an STD.

To learn more about the different types of STDs, read "Sexually Transmitted Diseases" at the back of this book. Many STDs have consequences that will last the rest of your life; they may affect your ability to have children; and they may even be fatal. It is very important to know how common STDs have become in today's society.

Oral and Anal Sex

Myth 5: Oral sex and anal sex aren't really sex.

The Facts: Yes, they are really sexual acts. **Oral sex** and anal sex are terms used to describe sexual acts that may bring a person to orgasm in ways outside of God's design for the union of male and female. God's design of how the male and females bodies fit together is a good and purposeful design. The consequences of sin often lead humans to distort or manipulate God's design for our own sinful pleasure.

Many teens believe that oral and anal sex are not the same as sexual intercourse, and so they believe they remain virgins even while doing these acts. However, this attitude ignores the truth of God's design for sexuality and the consequences of such acts. Although both of these activities avoid the risk of pregnancy, they are in fact sexual acts.

Those in dating relationships should avoid these and all other sexual acts that go against God's good design for sexuality. As always, if you're having sex before marriage, think of how sharing oral or anal sex will affect your relationship! There's nothing "casual" or "impersonal" about any sexual intimacy. It is never easy to end a dating relationship, and whether you engage in these sex acts or actual intercourse with someone other than your wife, the emotional impact will be there.

Sexual intercourse is about trust and intimacy. It is difficult to just "walk away" from someone with whom you have shared this type of physical intimacy. As you continue to mature physically, it is important to also grow spiritually through worship, Bible study, and prayer. Allowing the Word of God to inform your decisions about how you behave and act in intimate matters is a part of this spiritual maturation.

Cohabitation

Myth 6: Living together outside of marriage isn't really all that bad, right? Plenty of people seem to be doing it.

The Facts: Living together outside of marriage clearly disregards God's design for marriage and sexuality. God's will for a happy and fulfilling life makes no room for sexual relationships outside of marriage. Living together, or cohabitation, disregards the commitment to each other that God designed for the institution of marriage. **Fornication** (sexual relationships outside of marriage) dishonors both God the Creator and the men and women who freely take part in it.

The argument that living together gives a man and woman the opportunity to test out whether they would be compatible in marriage has been shown to be scientifically unsupported. Research has shown statistically that couples who live together before marriage are more likely to divorce than those who do not.

Cohabitation also harms relationships in the following ways:

1. People who cohabit before marriage exhibit a greater difficulty with solving problems than those who don't.

2. Cohabiting leads to more individualistic attitudes and behaviors, which work against a healthy marriage where two people must submit to each other in love.

3. Cohabiting actually convinces young people that relationships are fragile and temporary, thus making them more accepting of the idea of divorce.

4. Domestic violence is higher in cohabiting relationships than among married couples.

5. Cohabitants experience more drunkenness and depression than married couples.

6. People in cohabiting relationships are more likely to be unfaithful to their partners than married couples.

Contrary to what the culture would have you believe, research shows that the benefits of God's design for marriage cannot be replaced by sinful and self-serving relationships that refuse the lifelong commitment and vows that are a part of marriage.

Virginity

Myth 7: If you lose your virginity, it can be restored.

The Facts: God's design is for men and women to reserve acts of sexual intimacy for their spouse. Once men and women have taken part in sexual activities reserved for marriage, they have lost their virginity.

Some people stay virgins until they are married but are filled with sexually impure thoughts and desires that they do not try to control. Others may have lost their virginity but have repented and desire to remain chaste. God wants our thoughts, desires, and behaviors to be sexually pure, but none of us has lived perfectly.

In one way or another, everyone has disobeyed God's will with regard to sexuality. Impure sexual thoughts as well as sinful attitudes and actions all fall under God's judgment and condemnation. Thank God He has sent His Son to earn forgiveness for all sins, including those involving our sexuality.

Through the power of His Holy Spirit, God has given us the desire and ability to begin again as new people, forgiven and holy in the sight of God and eager to live for Him. St. Paul writes in 2 Corinthians 5:14–15, "For the love of Christ controls us, because we have concluded this: that one has died for all, therefore all have died; and He died for all, *that those who live might no longer live for themselves but for Him who for their sake died and was raised*" (emphasis added).

We find joy and fulfillment in showing love to others. We will not be content when we live for ourselves and seek to satisfy our own desires. Satisfaction comes when we love others unconditionally, not looking to see what we'll get out of the relationship and not loving someone only if they'll do the things we want. True contentment comes only from Jesus, who unconditionally loves us and unselfishly gave His life for us on the cross. Grace is undeserved love! How comforting it is to know that we are loved for who we are, as children of God, not for what we do or don't do.

Alan Long
Praying before the game!

© iStock.com / Michael

© iStock.com / Steve Debenport

Michael Plainer
Hanging with friends.

The Challenges of Becoming a Man

By God's Design Devotion

Read Ephesians 6:11–20.

"Take up the shield of faith, with which you can extinguish all the flaming darts of the evil one; and take the helmet of salvation, and the sword of the Spirit, which is the word of God, praying at all times in the Spirit" (Ephesians 6:16–18).

Who are you? What makes you who you are? The world has a lot of ideas. It likes to say you are defined by how tough you are. It defines you by what activities you enjoy, like football or getting lots of girls. It defines you by the mistakes you make and the tragedies you experience. It decides who you are based on things outside yourself.

However, the world doesn't get the last word. God says that your toughness shouldn't be based on external things. Instead, your toughness comes because you are a man of faith, with a shield and a sword from God. You are who you are because God has equipped you with armor that eyes cannot see. Jesus redeemed you by His suffering and death, and He defeated the devil by rising from the dead. In your Baptism, God called you His son and set you free from the lies of the devil and the world.

May you always find your identity as a man of faith in God, your Creator, Redeemer, and Sanctifier.

Prayer: God, thank You for making me a man of faith in You. Help me to always wear the armor of faith in service to others, praying always to the Spirit to help me. In Jesus' name. Amen.

Have you ever stopped to think what it means to be a young man in today's culture? It's an important question—so important, in fact, that much of your life will depend on how you answer it.

45

Our culture has its own ideas of what it means to be a man. If you watch popular TV shows, you might get the idea that being a man often means having sex with a lot of women to prove your sexual prowess. The media also depicts men as unemotional, self-interested, and ruthlessly ambitious in their workplace. If you listen to popular music, you'll hear that being a man often disrespects women as persons, desiring only their bodies and the satisfaction they can bring you. And if you play a lot of video games, you might think that women should be shaped like those fictional characters and that they are aggressive and in competition with you.

As you think about the cultural messages you receive about what it means to be a man, perhaps it would be helpful to think of a Christian man you respect or admire. What attitudes does this man (your father, a pastor, an uncle, a teacher) have that you respect? How do you think he developed these admirable attitudes? Is he responsible in his job? Is he gracious and kind toward women? What is his attitude toward God?

In the following sections, take a moment to examine the influence of culture on your perceptions of sexuality and what it means to be a young man.

Sexuality in the Media

Consider the influence of media. How many TV programs show strong, loving parents who take an active interest in their children? How many movies show faithful husbands and wives who don't sleep around or single people, especially men, who wait until they are married to have sex? How does popular music treat the topic of sexuality?

What attitudes about sex do you see reflected in

- the books or magazines you read or look at?
- the movie you saw most recently?
- your favorite TV show?
- the songs you listen to?
- the images you see on the Internet?
- the exaggerated figures of men and women in video games?

Do these show responsible, sexual persons who, though imperfect and vulnerable, have a set of values? Or do they picture unrealistic images of how men look, talk, and behave? Do the stories tell of trust, communication, and caring between two loving people? Or do they emphasize physical attraction and lack of commitment as being the best way to enjoy life?

Most of the media in our culture seems to be aimed at the lowest level of maturity and intelligence. If we constantly fill our minds with words and pictures that show sex as a casual or impersonal act, we may find it hard to maintain our own moral values and to develop lasting, loving relationships.

On the other hand, we can learn from those media that honestly describe a growing relationship between two real people, even if those people act in ways we might disagree with. We can learn that people get hurt in casual sexual relationships, that a woman's body should be valued and cherished no matter what its size, and that men can be thoughtful caretakers and providers. Sometimes the best example is a bad example. Be critical with the media that you view and listen to. Compare it with God's design for you as a young Christian man, and let God's Word remain your guide for decisions.

The Subtle Media Messages

What movies or TV shows have you seen that imply that sex outside of marriage is okay because everybody does it?

What effect might this subtle message have on a person who has not thought through his own values?

Have you ever heard the statement "sex sells"? Does it help to explain why sexy women are found in so many advertisements, TV shows, and movies? The images of sex influence how you think about women, yourself, and the products you want to buy.

Now ask yourself an important question again, and answer it honestly: how much has the culture influenced how you understand sexuality?

You may think it hasn't influenced you very much. In fact, most young people don't think they personally are very affected by the media they consume. But most of them believe their friends are *very* influenced by culture. Studies show that even young adults into their midtwenties are significantly impacted by the sex shown in the media.

If our ideas about sex can be so influenced by culture, perhaps our understanding of what it means to be a man can be similarly influenced.

Don't think so? It is now becoming common among young people to serial date, moving from one girlfriend to another with no real objective for long-term commitment or marriage. Another common practice is to just "hook up," to have a single interaction for the sole purpose of sexual pleasure. Even Christian young adults often delay marriage in order to live the casual single lifestyle longer. Is that your goal, to spend years casually having sex, or to move from one girlfriend to the next when you grow up? Or do you desire a committed, lifelong relationship with a woman who loves you for all your good qualities and forgives you for your weaknesses? Thinking about what you hope to have in a future relationship may help you better cope with pressure that says you need to have sex now or that this girl is good enough for now.

Our Culture's Message about Lifestyle Acceptance

What if I feel same-sex attraction?
Does that mean I'm gay?

Many young people worry unnecessarily about **homosexual** tendencies they suspect in themselves or about homosexual behavior in their past. They may have had one or more experiences with somebody of the same sex in which touching or other sexual interaction occurred. These experiences do not mean that someone is **gay**, **lesbian**, or **bisexual**.

It is also normal to have a deep attachment of friendship to someone of the same sex. David and Jonathan (see 1 Samuel 18), for instance, had a sincere love for each other that was very different from their normal sexual interest in the women they loved.

Many young people admire teachers or others who are the same sex. It is normal to admire someone very much and want to be near that person. Often, this admiration helps you discover a vocational direction you would like your own life to take.

Young people should not label themselves as homosexual. If you are worried about this, first share your concerns with your Father in heaven. Ask God to help you develop a healthy sense of identity rooted and grounded in Him, not in attractions or feelings that you have. Then, talk to your parents, a pastor, or another adult about your feelings.

It often takes a long time for a young person to feel at ease with members of the other sex. Be patient with yourself. Remember that you are not the only one who fears rejection; others feel just as insecure as you do. Ask God to help you become more comfortable with your own sexuality and with your own masculinity. He will help you.

What is homosexuality?

Homosexuality is a broad term that covers a lot of areas, everything from having sexual attractions toward the same sex to engaging in sexual behavior with the same sex and taking on a gay or lesbian identity. Many people with same-sex attractions or behavior decide not to call themselves gay or lesbian. Some people have same-sex attractions or behavior for periods of time, and then the attractions diminish or end. Many people who have same-sex attractions choose, with God's help, not to engage in sexual activity that violates His Word. They choose to live chastely, even if they continue to struggle with same-sex attractions.

What does the Bible say about homosexuality?

The Bible clearly states that intimate sexual expression is intended between one man and one woman within the marriage relationship. Men and women are complementary, and when they come together in marriage, they become one flesh where there is the possibility of procreation. Two men or two women together do not have this physical fitting together, and there is no possibility for procreation. Romans 1 teaches that homosexual behavior is one of the results of human sinfulness. Nowhere in the Bible is there any approval for homosexual behavior or same-sex marriage.

The Bible teaches that homosexual behavior (and any other sexual sin) is contrary to God's Word and His will. Whatever the cause, and even if a person's sexual orientation is not a deliberate choice, homosexual orientation is not a part of God's design.

While we as Christians cannot condone homosexual behavior, we want to show compassion and love toward those who struggle with same-sex attraction. We can minister to those struggling with homosexuality with patience and compassion, in the love and Spirit of Christ, who says, "Neither do I condemn you; go, and from now on sin no more" (John 8:11).

As Christians, we need to be aware of our treatment of people with same-sex attraction, especially with more and more social acceptance of homosexuality and more legal recognition of same-sex marriage. There are other consequences for those struggling with same-sex attraction. Despite the media's portrayal of wide acceptance of homosexual lifestyles, young adults who struggle with same-sex attraction still experience high levels of rejection and are more likely to have high levels of depression, to have attempted suicide, and to use illegal drugs.

As Christians, we must avoid hurtful or mean behavior toward those who might be struggling with this issue. Sometimes other students are labeled "gay" or "lesbian" because of their appearance or because their interests are different from the norm. Such labels can follow a person for years and influence how he or she is treated by others. As Christians, we will avoid name-calling, gossip, bullying, and harassment. We need to treat others as we would like others to treat us (Matthew 7:12).

We need to show compassion to those who are hurting and struggling with their feelings. The redeeming love of Christ, which rescues humanity from sin and the power of the devil, is offered to all through repentance and faith in Jesus, regardless of the nature of a person's sinfulness. We can proclaim to those struggling with homosexuality that God forgives all sin for Christ's sake and makes possible a new life through the power of the Holy Spirit. In fact, Scripture talks about those who used to act homosexually but have been washed, sanctified, and justified by God's Spirit (see 1 Corinthians 6:9–11). God can rescue people from homosexual practice! Christ's love and strength can help a person abstain from sexual sins. The person struggling in this area cannot change by their own strength, but they can rely on God's power to be **celibate** (abstain from sexual relations).

Is there a gay gene?

For years, people have claimed 10 percent of the population is gay, and in recent years, as our society has pushed for acceptance and tolerance of everyone's lifestyles, the public's perception is even higher. In 2002, a Gallup poll found that those surveyed believed that 21 percent of men are gay and 22 percent of women are lesbians. That's at least one in every five people! We now know, however, that despite perception and publicity, the number is somewhere between 1 and 3.5 percent. The 2000 U.S. Census Bureau found that homosexual couples constitute less than

1 percent of American households. A more recent study shows that 3.5 percent of Americans label themselves as gay, lesbian, or bisexual.

The American Psychological Association admits that there is no consensus among scientists about the exact reasons that an individual develops a certain sexual orientation. They do conclude that most people experience little or no sense of choice about their sexual orientation. About 88 percent of gay men and 68 percent of lesbians perceived that they had little or no choice about the existence of personal homosexual feelings.

Studies have shown that homosexuality runs in families, which led many researchers to assume a genetic link to homosexuality. However, despite many studies done to search for a genetic connection, no gene for homosexuality has been found.

There are some common factors for many people with same-sex attractions. Some people with same-sex attractions grew up not acting like or feeling connected to their same-sex peers. Some report early, inappropriate exposure to sex or pornography as children. Others report feeling disconnected from their same-sex parent or siblings.

There is a strong link between childhood behaviors and adult behaviors. The more a child views same-sex relationship behaviors in people significant to his or her development, the more likely he or she will exhibit homosexual orientation in their adulthood.

Humans are not like machines that can be programmed to act in certain ways. There is always an element of choice or free will in human behavior—including human sexual behavior. Choosing to "come out" or act on homosexual desires develops from a complex interaction among a person's temperament, environment, relationships, experiences, perceptions, and choices—and from the fact that we live in a fallen world. So each person's sexual development is different.

Can a person change from homosexuality to heterosexuality?

What we do know, from many testimonies and studies, is that some people do change their sexual behaviors. For some, homosexuality is a changeable condition, and people who overcome same-sex attraction should be allowed to change to live the way God intended. God uses many different means to help people change. The Holy Spirit works through the Means of Grace—the Word of God and the Sacraments—to strengthen us. He gives prayer, self-control, accountability, healthy relationships, therapy, worship, confession, and assurance of our forgiveness as tools to bring healing and change in people's lives. Jesus' victory over sin is our victory over sin. His Word is powerful!

The goal for those struggling with same-sex attractions should not be **heterosexuality**, but holiness. Those who feel attracted to members of the same sex can consider whether they are pursuing their sexual desires or pursuing peace through Christ. Trusting in the Lord and turning away from temptation brings complete wholeness and well-being (Proverbs 3:5–8, 15). Some people may never feel released from same-sex attraction, but they can continue to walk through life in sexual purity, lifted up by God's grace and forgiveness.

What does it mean to be transgendered?

Our culture tends to use many terms loosely and interchangeably, but sometimes this creates confusion. For example, some people use the terms *sex* and *gender* as if they have the same meaning. This isn't precisely true. The term *sex* is a way to designate the biological fact that we are male or female. *Gender* often describes how a person feels about his or her sex. That is, it is a term related to self-perception. Anywhere you go, biological sex differences remain the same, but gender roles, behaviors, and attributes can be different depending on the culture. What culture (or a larger group) believes is appropriate for males and females can differ from group to group or society to society.

What makes this especially confusing is that some people in our culture today don't like the basic male and female distinctions in sex and are working to create many new genders. Some say there are seven genders, and others as many as fifty-six! But if gender describes how people perceive themselves, they can also be confused about this. If a man believes himself to be a woman, some may say he has "gender identity disorder," which is a psychological condition.

Another term to describe this condition is **transgender**, which means that a person does not identify with his or her biological sex. Society today is moving away from seeing a transgender condition as a disorder and more to celebrating a person for however he thinks of himself. There are several different ways people express themselves as transgender.

A **transsexual** person tries to look, dress, and act like a member of the opposite sex. They may have been born male, but they think of themselves as female. They may even have operations to remove their biological sex organs and have sex organs of the opposite sex created instead.

Transvestites, or people who cross-dress, are usually comfortable with the sex God created them to be, but they like to wear clothing that is typically worn by the opposite sex.

Not all people who seem genderless—having neither specifically masculine nor specifically feminine characteristics, also called **androgynous**—are transgender persons.

Sexuality in the Workplace

What about sexual harassment?

The law says that no one, man or woman, has to put up with unwelcome sexual advances, requests for sexual favors, and other unwanted verbal or physical conduct of a sexual nature.

The sexual harassment law is aimed mostly at the workplace, but the courts have said that it also applies to schools when the behavior causes a student fear, anxiety, shame, or embarrassment or keeps the student from being able to attend school.

Does that mean it's against the law for a man to flirt with a woman?

It is not against the law to flirt. However, you do need to be aware of how your flirting is being received by a young woman. Is the flirting unwelcome? Did she ask you to stop? Did you continue flirting even after she let you know she doesn't welcome it? Might you be making school or work an uncomfortable place for her? If this kind of flirting happens at a party rather than at school or work, it's probably not illegal—but it's still wrong. When a young woman requests you to stop flirting or if you see you are making her nervous or uncomfortable, you must stop. Apologize to her and perhaps talk about other things that may interest both of you—things that do not include sexual innuendo.

What about the woman who leads a man on and then rejects him?

Both men and women need to be aware of the signals they are sending to others. What you see as flirting from a young woman may just be how she shows kindness or general interest in you as a person. She may not be flirting with sexual interest in mind. Even if she is flirting with you, it is not okay for you to expect physical intimacy or force it on her. She may not be fully aware of the effect her flirting is having on you. If you feel her flirting is causing you to become lustful or aggressive toward her, you can kindly ask what she means by her flirting. You can then share with her your values about sexuality—that it is a struggle as a young man, but that you respect her enough to ask her to stop. You can apologize for the misunderstanding and clearly set your boundaries. Who knows? She just might start to view you in a new light as a Christian young man!

But what if a person gets so "excited" that he can't stop himself ?

That myth is popular among people who do not want to accept responsibility for their own actions. Controlling one's sexual drive is possible at any point from first arousal to orgasm. If you are alone with a young woman and begin to feel that your sexual desire is becoming overwhelming, step away from the situation to cool down. Then explain to the young woman why you had to step away—not to reject her, but to respect her and to control yourself.

What's the difference between joking around about sex and sexual harassment? Everybody tells sexual jokes sometimes.

If it feels like harassment to the victim, it has gone beyond joking. This involves one person setting an expectation that if they do something for you sexually, then you will do something else that helps them (a promotion, a raise, a better grade). It is also harassment if someone feels the situation has become hostile, that they are no longer able to work or study in an environment where they feel safe. Sexual harassment often leaves people feeling very depressed, afraid, and unable to trust others. Many students report that they no longer want to come to school after it has happened.

A nationwide survey of high school students found that 85 percent of girls and 76 percent of boys reported being sexually harassed at school. Unwanted sexual comments, jokes, gestures, or looks were the most common forms of harassment. Surveys show that 65 percent of girls and 42 percent of boys also have experienced unwelcome sexual touching, pinching, or grabbing.

Talk to an adult you trust at your school if this type of harassment is occurring there. Talk to a manager at work if the harassment is occurring between you and a co-worker. It is a serious charge, but it is also seriously wrong for this type of behavior to take place at school or work. Clear communication, modest behavior, and firm boundaries are the best prevention.

The Not-Subtle Message of Pornography

Some of the most beautiful statues or pictures portray the naked human body. They give us an appreciation for how wonderfully God has made us. Unfortunately, humans take this beauty and distort it. We create, produce, or view images of the naked human body that are not good.

If when you look at a picture (or statue or piece of art) you can easily remember that it shows a special person who is valued by God, this is not pornography. If you do not appreciate the beauty of God's design when you look at the image, then it is pornography.

Pornography is created when a human is displayed as a sex object, a thing to be used for someone else's pleasure. Pornography uses human sexuality as a tool to cause people to lust, crave, and imagine themselves doing sexual acts with the person depicted in the image. Once you have used pornography to bring pleasure to yourself, you usually feel shame or guilt, and with good reason. It is wrong for anyone to manipulate the human body in this way for sexual gratification. Instead of being grateful that God has made us male and female so that someday you can enjoy full sexual pleasure in marriage, pornography makes you limit and hide that sexual pleasure in your own private space.

Pornography also makes sex something public and unspecial because the images are shared with faceless, nameless viewers. Might it help for you to think that the people shown in those images are individuals whom God created, for whom Jesus died, and for whom the Holy Spirit desires that they lead godly lives? They are indeed God's creation, as you are.

Pornography, whether found on the Internet, cable TV, or in photographs and magazines, surrounds you, and the temptation is always there. How can you resist?

By the grace and power of God!

It will not be an easy temptation for you to overcome, but there are things you can do. You can remember always that the Holy Spirit gives you power to resist temptation and to exercise self-control. Remember that your body and the bodies of others are the gifts of God. You can be aware that such pornographic materials exist, yet you can avoid them.

You can also avoid those situations that might pull you into groups whose actions and words degrade sex and the human body. You can seek the support and encouragement of other young people who share your love of Jesus and desire to live according to God's design for you. You can pray daily for strength to resist the pressure to be like the culture that surrounds you and says that pornography is okay. The Bible says: "Do not be conformed to this world, but be transformed by the renewal of your mind, that by testing you may discern what is the will of God, what is good and acceptable and perfect" (Romans 12:2).

Is it really wrong to just look? How can a picture, magazine, or movie hurt me?

Consider where your Christian attitudes, opinions, and values come from. You weren't born with them. Indeed, God's Word reminds us that sin so deeply infects us that we naturally choose sinful things. Paul writes, "Put off your old self, which belongs to your former manner of life and is corrupt through deceitful desires" (Ephesians 4:22). On the basis of the Bible, we call this "our old sinful flesh."

We know, too, from God's Word that the devil seeks to work through the world—the evil influences all around us—to lead God's people to sin and lack of trust in God. Peter tells us, "Be sober-minded; be watchful. Your adversary the devil prowls around like a roaring lion, seeking someone to devour" (1 Peter 5:8).

In Baptism, God made us His own children—forgiven people who are given the power to resist our own sinful desires, the devil, and the sinful world.

The question then becomes quite simple: is pornography part of the world, which appeals to our sinful flesh, or is it part of God's good creation, which appeals to us as children of God? It isn't both!

While pornography may seem exciting and thrilling, especially at first, it can pollute our minds in the same way sewage pollutes a river. Many young people are finding themselves psychologically addicted to Internet pornography without realizing how they got there. Because their minds were still forming when pornography polluted them, they have difficulty healing the way their brain was trained to think of sexuality. If you are in such a situation, seek out your pastor, your Christian friends, and a trained Christian counselor immediately.

Viewing pornography now, while your brain is still developing, may impact your sexual experiences for years to come, perhaps even your entire life. One way to look at it is that by viewing pornography, you are "teaching" your body about sexuality—but in an unhealthy, selfish way. Your brain may become wired to expect an unnatural stimulus in order for your body to be aroused and satisfied. And the images you see now cannot simply be "erased" from your mind whenever you want. These images will remain in your mind and imagination. When you look at your future wife, will you see her and her alone? Do you see how this may affect your future marriage?

What if someone sends me nude pictures and I didn't even want them?

Exposing someone to nudity used to be called flashing. *Flasher* is a slang word for **exhibitionist**, a person who gets sexual satisfaction from showing his or her **genitals** to others. The typical flasher used to be a man who delighted in shocking young girls in public. These types of exhibitionists do still exist, and they should be reported to the police.

However, with the easy access to digital photography, live Internet chat forums, and social media, exhibitionists have new ways to expose themselves to people. It is important that you know these risks and what to do when exhibitionists expose themselves to you through digital media.

First, if someone asks if they can send nude photos of themselves or share other sexual content with you, say no. And while it may be difficult to go to your parents, it is important that they know this has happened. If this was the first time, you were probably quite shocked and upset. This type of exposure is not your fault, though, and you should not feel guilty about it.

Second, understand that many of the people you may talk or interact with through the Internet or through video game chats are still people you do not know. You would not invite a stranger to come into your living room and just start talking with you about sex. You should not allow people you meet in the digital world to do that either. Ultimately, you are in control, even if that means just hitting the power button.

As you get older, you might find that friends or acquaintances want to share nude or sexually explicit images of themselves or others with you. You may think this is funny or harmless, but the pictures they are sending are not something to dismiss or laugh about. They may show individuals who have not consented to having their photograph taken or shared. Or they may be people who are being paid to make illegal pornographic images. Exhibitionists and those who want to shock you with sexually explicit images are violating basic respect for other human beings. They are also dismissing God's good design for sexuality, making it public, cheap, and something that others may laugh about. As a young Christian man, you can choose not to participate in receiving or sharing these types of digital images. Further, as a teen who is growing into adulthood, you hold the distinct vocation to protect and care for those around you. Resisting sexual temptation now equips you to be the man that God designed you to be, to care for others in His creation.

Other Things You Might Want to Know

What is incest?

Incest is having sexual relations with a member of your family or another close relative. It is a crime. Many incidents of incest take place as a form of sexual abuse. Usually, an older relative will convince a younger person that this form of sex is okay or that any guilt belongs to the younger person. This is a betrayal of trust and is never true. The victim is not guilty and may suffer severe physical, spiritual, and psychological damage because of the abuse.

He or she should firmly resist any future advances and should report the problem to a parent, pastor, or other trusted counselor. The victim of incest needs help, and so does the aggressor.

What is a prostitute?

A prostitute is a person who engages in sexual activity for money or other goods, such as drugs or shelter. Most prostitutes are women; most customers are men.

There is a common but dangerous myth that most prostitutes have freely chosen to sell their bodies. Research shows that most have been physically forced or psychologically manipulated into prostitution. If a woman is forced into sex work, then she is a victim. Prostituted women (or men) may have a history of homelessness, mental health issues, incarceration, emotional/physical/sexual abuse, or drug use. The use of violence to enslave girls or women for sex trafficking is not uncommon, but the traffickers also use psychological control over these women who often see no way out of their situation.

When a person is coerced, forced, or deceived into starting or continuing in prostitution, that person is a victim of sex trafficking. Anyone involved in recruiting, harboring, transporting, providing, or obtaining a person for that purpose is responsible for trafficking crimes. Many women and girls are forced to continue in prostitution because of an unlawful "debt" (supposedly incurred through their sale and transportation) that the perpetrator says they must pay off before they can be free.

As a godly young man, regularly pray for the victims of sex trafficking and those continuing in prostitution. Pray that these women would find a means of escape from prostitution and hear from those concerned about their true value as children of God, not as sexual objects. Pray that their situations would change and that others would love them for who they are, not for what they can do for someone else. Pray that the men involved would recognize and repent of their sin and understand that their sexual desires must be controlled.

A Review of God's Design: It's All about Serving

Let's go back to the beginning and review this book's lessons in light of your being set apart by God to become a Christian man.

From the very beginning, it is clear that God made us for relationships with Him and with other people. Review the Genesis account of creation if you doubt this statement. Next, examine your life to see if you daily rely on God and His promises to help you grow into that Christian man. Do you still sin every day? (We all do!) Do you still read God's Word in the Bible? (It is where our faith is nurtured and strengthened.) Do you still cling to the forgiveness that Christ won for you on the cross? These are the basics of how God remains central in your life as you grow up: recognizing your sin, receiving Christ's forgiveness, and reading and hearing the Word of God on your own *and* at your church.

If you feel distant from God or don't spend time in prayer, worship, and Bible reading, you may find yourself growing apart from God, thinking that Jesus was "just a kid thing." But distancing yourself from God is also likely to affect your decisions about relationships with other people. The Lutheran theologian Dietrich Bonhoeffer said that we are never as close to another person as when we approach him or her through Christ.

By this, Bonhoeffer meant that when the people you are close to are also close to Christ, you share a communion with them in Christ. Together you are a part of Christ's one Body. Can it get closer than that—to be part of the same body? (Doesn't this sound like the one-flesh union we talked about earlier?)

When you share the same belief in Christ, the same values for Christian living, and the same need for forgiveness, your closeness to other people will be as close to God's design for human fellowship as it can be. Even if you never marry, you and your fellow members in the Body of Christ will together honor God and one another because your decisions and choices will be led by God's Word.

Looking back to our creation by God, another point becomes clear. In being made for others, we are called not to selfishness, but to service. God calls men and women to serve each other, not to take advantage of each other. St. Paul describes it this way in Ephesians 5:22–25: "Wives, submit to your own husbands, as to the Lord . . . [a]s the church submits to *Christ*" and "Husbands, love your wives as *Christ* loved the church and gave Himself up for her" (emphasis added). Christ is the essential person in both of these statements. The submission that occurs in marriage, and in the Body of Christ, is not about coercion and control; it is about service. A wife serves her husband because her husband serves her. A husband sacrifices for his wife because Christ sacrificed Himself for the Church. Service and sacrifice are at the heart of God's love for us.

Reading the Gospels, we can see that Jesus' chief characteristic was love through service to His Father and to us. Love gives itself to others; it does not take from them. It seems that many cultural messages have twisted this eternal truth. Being a strong man has been distorted, and many view a strong man as being in a position to control or dominate others. But a strong Christian man understands he is a servant to all, just as Jesus was a servant to you.

Jesus gave Himself for you, even to the point of death on a cross. As a child of God and as a Christian man, you will serve others in many self-sacrificing ways that put other people before you. Consider simply treating others with common courtesy. Opening a door to allow others to go before you requires putting yourself last. Managing employees at work involves serving them and making sure they have what they need to get their jobs done. Caring for your wife and children will mean putting their needs before yours. But that's okay, because your Christian wife will always be striving to put your needs before hers. God does have a beautiful design for marriage because husband and wife are both served.

How does this look in intimate relationships you may want to have right now as a young, single Christian man? You may have strong sexual desires for your girlfriend, but serving her in love requires that you put those desires aside until marriage. In such cases, you together decide to value sexual purity and decency above your own desires. Many people do not act this way now and end up bringing self-serving attitudes into marriage with them.

Do you imagine that once you are married, you can then have everything you want? Serving your wife in marriage means that you continue that same self-giving love. The mutual love of marriage involves each of you giving yourself to the other. Because of sin, you may have to struggle to keep from viewing your wife as someone who should give you whatever you ask or from selfishly just wanting to take care of yourself. Christ's love is the model for the love we are to have toward our spouse: love that does not depend on the other doing anything or being anything; love that doesn't demand an exchange and does not have to be earned by your wife in any way.

Finally, another important lesson to review is repentance. God demands perfection from us, but we are not and never will be perfect. A quick reading of the Ten Commandments quickly tells us we don't love God with our *whole* heart, nor do we love our neighbors as much as we love ourselves. Repentance is recognizing our sinful hearts *and* the daily sins we commit by failing to do good things and easily doing selfish things. But God gave us His own Son, Jesus, to be perfect in our place because we could never be perfect. And because Jesus was perfect (without sin), and because He died on the cross, He took the punishment for us as sinful people. When Jesus rose from the dead on Easter morning, He even conquered death. We have Jesus with us in this life to help us, and we will be with Jesus forever after we die. This is a great and wonderful thing that brings us thankful hearts. We now daily live to love God and serve the people around us.

Jesus Demonstrated God's Love

Above all, remember that your identity as a man is not in the things you may own or desire but in Christ alone. Through Jesus, you have been adopted into God's own family forever. You are Jesus' brother and a man of God.

The Millers

My wife loves my dinner!

While Jesus was here on earth, He demonstrated that God loves us in a very personal way. A leper, Levi the tax collector, a widow, Simon the Pharisee, a prostitute—Jesus loved and forgave all these sinners. He loves and forgives you too.

How many teachers today would bother having class if there was a big snowstorm and only one student was there? Not many. Yet, if you page through the Gospel of Luke, you'll notice that Jesus spent a lot of His time teaching or healing just one person. He came to seek the lost sheep, the sinner who had strayed from God's care. He seeks you also when you stray, and He calls you back to Him. Listen to Him!

Perhaps you have not been pure with a young woman in the past—or even now. Are you sorry? Have you stopped listening to the Good Shepherd calling you? If you are not sorry or have not apologized to God, you are in rebellion against God. Maybe you have tried to stop, but you keep falling back into your sin and are worried God won't forgive you.

When you share problems and challenges with God, remember that you are very special in His sight. Incredible though it seems, you have His undivided attention. You don't have to do anything or be anything to get Him to love you. He just does—and He always will. "He who did not spare His own Son but gave Him up for us all, how will He not also with Him graciously give us all things?" (Romans 8:32).

The best thing He graciously gives you is forgiveness!

Trusting in Christ. Faithful. Special in God's sight. Self-controlled. Keep these qualities in mind as you read the following chapters dealing more specifically with navigating dating and relationships.

Mom . . . She said yes to church and dinner on Sunday.

Sis, volunteering at the soup kitchen on our first date!

Dating 5

Read 1 John 4:13–19.

"We love because He first loved us" (1 John 4:19).

When young men hear the word *love*, it doesn't always mean the same thing that it does to young women. It is a word that many young men just don't want to hear, especially from a girlfriend. You may feel that *love* means commitment, and you are just too young for that kind of serious relationship. This is the time for you to have fun, not love.

God has a different idea about love. God's love for us means He sent His Son to be your Savior from sin. Love is what God showed you in your Baptism, when He made you part of His family. Love binds you to God in Christ. Love casts out fear. And you love others because God loved you first.

You may not be ready for the serious commitment of romantic love, but the love of God equips you to love others by showing respect, strength, and compassion to them at all times.

Prayer: Dear God, thank You for the love You showed me in Jesus. Thank You for giving me faith in You through my Baptism. Help me to always look for love in You and to point others to Your love. Amen.

Dating

Now that you've thought about God's design for marriage and sexuality and how to grow into an adult Christian man, you can apply this knowledge to dating.

Have you ever asked yourself any of the following questions?

Does a person have to date to be considered normal?

How do I get started dating?

Is dating only one person a good idea?

What is the best way to handle a breakup?

How much physical contact is okay?

What if we've already had intercourse?

Most of your dating questions will give you an opportunity to apply God's design for sexuality in your life as a young Christian man. Maybe the very first question to consider is this:

What will a young Christian woman be looking for in a man she would like to date?

She will look for a Christian, kind, modest, thoughtful, loving young man who values and respects her and who does not try to manipulate or take advantage of her. Does this describe you?

Kindness

How can I be more kind?

It may seem like the popular kids in school are the ones having all the fun and doing all the dating. Many young people find that just being kind to others brings a popularity that is very rewarding. By making a decision to be kind to everyone, you communicate your appreciation for every individual. You learn about the differences that people have, and you enjoy what you learn about others. It teaches you about yourself. It helps you identify the characteristics in other people that make you comfortable and relaxed, and it helps you identify the people to whom you feel connected.

Being kind also means that you have a servant's heart. Through kindly serving others by being helpful with tasks, ready to work together, eager to talk with them about their interests, and listening and supporting them when they struggle, you will find that people are drawn to your kindness. A kind person is a great person to know. When you do this in order to serve them, your kindness will be genuine.

Modesty

Some girls dress so sexy. Don't they get it?
Don't they know what that does to me?

It is tempting for a girl to dress in a revealing way, flaunting her sexuality, in order to get noticed by boys. But a relationship based on being noticed for one's body only is troubled from the start. Some girls fail to serve young men when they don't consider the impact their choices and behavior have on others. Some choose clothing styles that increase your temptation to sin.

However, when you notice a girl's body, this does not excuse you from having lustful reactions. You are responsible for your own behavior.

Today's world is a hostile environment for Christians. Understand that the young women around you live in this same hostile culture. It takes integrity and commitment on your part as a young Christian man to make godly choices for a sexually pure and decent life and to encourage the young women you know to do the same by your example. This, too, will require the help of the Holy Spirit as you grow into the role of an adult Christian man who cares for those around him. Again, the Bible leads us not to conform to the world, but to be transformed (changed, made unique, dedicated). Romans 12:1–2 says, "I appeal to you . . . by the mercies of God, to present your bodies as a living sacrifice, holy and acceptable to God. . . . Do not be conformed to this world, but be transformed by the renewal of your mind."

Remember that the Bible doesn't make any moral distinction between men and women when it calls Christians to be lights in a dark world. How else will people come to know about Jesus, except from His people sharing His Word? And how interested will they be in what we have to say if we have a bad reputation? God holds males and females equally responsible and accountable for their thoughts, attitudes, and actions.

Clothing is a language that speaks a message. Young women want you to notice not their bodies, but who they are as people. They sometimes mistakenly use their bodies to get your attention first. It takes courage for young women to recognize and resist peer influences in order to find a modest style of outward appearance. It also takes courage for young men to resist similar peer influences and *not* look lustfully at young women who dress immodestly.

Remember that your value comes from being a loved child of God. You are so valuable to God that He gave up His only Son to save you and to make you His own! Treat young women with dignity, decency, courtesy, and respect because they belong to God. Finally, look to God to make you "strong and courageous. Do not be frightened, and do not be dismayed, for the LORD your God is with you wherever you go" (Joshua 1:9).

The Dating Scene

The following section presents a few different scenarios that you might be thinking about as a young Christian man. How does a young man talk to, act with, show interest in, and get to know the young woman he might want to date? Perhaps these scenes will help you as you think about your own behavior. Dating, at its heart, is the early stage of establishing a relationship that might lead to marriage. "Would I want to marry this young woman?" is always a good question to have in your mind. Dating should not be about what you can get: improved status with your peers, physical satisfaction, or other things. Dating is learning about the character and values of the young woman you initially find interesting or attractive. The attraction may be where it starts, but dating is to determine whether or not this young woman shares your Christian beliefs, respects God and others, understands what it means to serve others in kindness and thoughtfulness, and appreciates you (faults and all) as a Christian young man.

Scenario 1: I've been saying "Hi" all semester to a girl in my English class, but that's as far as it goes. How can I get to know her better?

Greeting someone with a big smile is a good start. Some days, try to leave class at the same time she does. Ask her a question about the homework assignment; tell her what you heard about the next test; joke with her. You might gradually become better friends. Then, one of you might suggest doing something together—maybe as a part of a larger group.

It could be, though, that as you get to know each other, you'll find you really don't have much in common. That's why it's smarter not to pin all your hopes on one person. Your best bet is to be open and talk to many different people.

Scenario 2: It took me weeks to work up courage enough to talk to this girl after class. She just said "I gotta go" and left. What's wrong with me?

Nothing is wrong with you. Chances are she may be as nervous speaking to you as you are to her. Speak to her in a group situation where she might feel more comfortable. If she still seems unfriendly, don't take it personally. Be patient with yourself and this whole situation of wanting to date someone. Focus on developing friendships first and not on looking for someone you want to date. Your goal is to find a young woman who is just as interested in getting to know you as you are in knowing her. Dating usually comes about as friendship matures into mutual attraction and respect.

Scenario 3: After six weeks of talking to a really cute girl after history class, I finally asked her on a date. It was a disaster; neither of us had a good time. What went wrong?

You probably didn't have enough in common to keep up an enjoyable conversation. Next time, get to know someone you feel more comfortable with, a young woman who has first become your friend. If you don't know any girls that well, look for a group of guys and girls who do things together. Check out extracurricular clubs at school or volunteer groups; don't be afraid to try something new!

Scenario 4: Is there anything wrong with going out on a blind date?

Many successful marriages began with the introduction of a man and a woman by a person or couple known to both of them. Usually, however, people find it more comfortable to get to know someone in the company of mutual friends before spending time alone together on a date.

Scenario 5: What about hooking up?

"Hooking up" is not dating. The purpose of hooking up is to make out or have sex. Warnings against hooking up with someone you just met are the equivalent of warning young children not to go with strangers. The consequences can be just as traumatic. Though you may think you are a good judge of character, and though the other person may appear "cool" or "cute," first impressions often are incorrect.

Obviously, hooking up with a girl you don't know for the purpose of sexual activity disobeys God, just as it shows disrespect for the other person and for yourself. People who are willing to "hook up" or to be picked up want instant satisfaction. They seek "fun" on a one-night-stand basis, but it can be very dangerous, even life-threatening. Is this what you expect to do with young women?

It is never a good idea to approach a young woman just to see what you can get, especially if it is just sex. Such an approach is selfish and shows no respect for the young woman. Disrespecting another person also disrespects God and His will for His people.

Hooking up is not God's will for healthy relationships. Most hookups do not lead to a relationship. In fact, they purposefully avoid the work of a real relationship. They are a quick substitute for dating or courtship, and they only hurt, complicate, and confuse any friendships or acquaintances. If you are using, or plan to use, someone as "a friend with benefits," you are way off from God's will and design for sexuality.

You can exercise self-control. Avoid situations that increase temptations. Pray for God's Spirit to guide you. Remind yourself of God's design for sexuality—and the good reasons He has for restricting sexual intercourse to marriage. It is to keep you safe, healthy, and a pure gift to give your future wife.

Scenario 6: Is there something wrong with me because I don't want to date?

Many young people do little or no dating during their teen years. These teens usually have friends of both sexes, and they spend time with their friends.

The group gets together for school sporting events, after-school clubs, video game playing—whatever. Sometimes closer friendships form within the group. People find others they can talk to and confide in. All these activities are actually wonderful ways to learn what characteristics you will want in a future wife.

The most interesting groups are very flexible about their membership. New people are welcome, and no one is pressured to participate in any one activity. Often one person will belong to several informal groups. It's a no-hassle way to become more comfortable with people of the other sex.

Scenario 7: My girlfriend's father won't let me come to their house when her parents aren't home. Why doesn't her father trust me?

Maybe he trusts your integrity and your dependability but is a little uneasy about your judgment in a situation that could be very tempting. Being alone with a person you like can be very exciting. It is very easy to let things go further than you intended. Your girlfriend's father was a young man once, too, and probably understands better than you that you shouldn't invite temptation. It will come all on its own!

Scenario 8: I didn't intend to go out only with Julia, but now everyone assumes we are a couple. We've gone out three weekends in a row. I don't want to hurt her, but I don't like this trapped feeling. How do I get out?

Take the risk of sharing your feelings with Julia. Be sure to make it clear that you really do enjoy her company. Maybe Julia has been feeling trapped too. The pressure to be "dating" someone can be pretty strong during this time. It is important to remember that your identity is not based on who you are dating, or even *if* you are dating. The decision to date is a serious one, requiring serious effort. If you are not ready for that right now, share that with your friend and encourage her also to be content with Christian fellowship and friendship.

Scenario 9: Sometimes dating can be a complete mess! I've even heard about girls getting raped by their dates. I don't ever *want to be accused of that. Is there a way I can help protect my friends who are girls?*

When dating, it's a good idea to spend most of your time in groups and with friends, especially as you just begin getting to know someone. Let your friends know the people you are spending time with and avoid those situations where someone you don't know may pose a risk. Avoid potentially harmful situations, and stay in control of your actions by avoiding substances like alcohol that impair judgment. Encourage your friends, both male and female, to do the same. You and your friends should always avoid parties where alcohol or drugs are involved.

You can also try to care for and protect others who may have had too much to drink or have otherwise put themselves in vulnerable situations. You can call their parents or otherwise help them get home safely.

A Christian young man will speak up when a situation is getting out of control at a social gathering or party. Be aware of who might be at risk. Report trouble to responsible people. Call security if you are on a college campus or the police if you are in a home or other public place. It is important to report crimes so that the perpetrators can be held accountable.

As your relationship with a young woman progresses, you can eventually discuss together your sexual limits before tempting situations occur. Learn what your date finds acceptable for intimacy and what is not comfortable for her, and respect that.

This is not a one-way street. As a young Christian man, you should know your intentions and discuss them with your girlfriend. Does she know what you value and what your limits are for physical touch and intimacy? By setting the example for communicating values and expectations, you earn the respect of the young woman you are dating.

As a young Christian man, you can also make sure your other male friends know the following:

- It is never okay to use force, coercion, alcohol, or drugs to pressure a woman into unwanted sexual contact. Such an act is a criminal offense.
- The amount of money you have spent on a woman entitles you to nothing.
- When a woman says no, she means no.
- No matter how aroused you or your date may get, you are both able to control your sexual behavior.
- If alcohol or drugs have removed your ability to think clearly and use good judgment, you are still responsible for your behavior.

Rape is a terrible sin. Although God forgives all sins, including those of a sexual assailant, the victim's emotional and mental scars do not go away. Moreover, the victim may be forced to cope with an unwanted pregnancy, and the sad reality is that many in this situation choose **abortion**.

Scenario 10: But what happens if a woman is raped, either by a stranger or someone she knows?

Rape happens when one person forces another to have sexual intercourse. Women and girls are usually the victims, although boys can be raped by either men or predatory women. Most psychologists feel that rape is a crime of violence and that a rapist wants to hurt and frighten a victim rather than get sexual pleasure.

A person who has been raped should go immediately to a hospital or a rape crisis center. A doctor will check her for injuries and will also look for evidence that the rape happened. In women, they look for sperm cells in the vagina. (No police report will be made without her consent. But if she delays or washes herself first, it may not be possible to prove anything.) The doctor also takes steps to prevent sexually transmitted disease.

The doctor also can recommend agencies that will provide free or inexpensive counseling. Victims need spiritual and emotional support as well as medical attention. A woman should seek help from her pastor or somebody she trusts as a committed Christian to receive the support in Christ that she needs.

Scenario 11: What is an "abusive relationship"?

People often remain in an abusive relationship because they see it as better than being alone. When self-esteem gets low enough, it's easy to say, "This is all I deserve. If we break up, I'll never find anyone else who will love me." They forget that they are special people who are loved and valued by God. God can and will provide the courage to break free, the patience to endure a period of being alone, and the confidence needed to form a healthy relationship with someone new.

An abusive relationship is one in which there is a pattern of repeated verbal, emotional, or physical abuse by which one dating partner tries to control the other. A woman might threaten to break up with her male friend if he doesn't give up his other friends and outside interests and spend all his free time with her. A man might insist on making all the decisions or threaten violence if his female friend won't have sex with him.

Once a person gives in to any of these kinds of emotional blackmail, it becomes harder to stand up for his or her rights the next time. The abuser continues to do whatever it takes to make the dating partner conform to his or her will.

If a woman allows a man to threaten violence or actually hurt her, that violence is likely to continue. There will be times when the abuser reforms and asks forgiveness, but he will almost always repeat the pattern of violence again. Only with outside help is the abuser likely to accept responsibility for his own behavior and learn new ways of dealing with stress and conflict.

Scenario 12: How can I tell if I'm in an abusive relationship?

Does your girlfriend

- ☐ get angry easily and often?
- ☐ handle anger by destroying things or treating people roughly?
- ☐ constantly put you down?
- ☐ hurt your feelings on purpose?
- ☐ frequently embarrass you in front of your friends?
- ☐ refuse to believe she has really hurt you?
- ☐ brag about previous boyfriends?

- ☐ insist on making all the decisions that affect both of you?
- ☐ demand to know where you are and who you've talked to on your phone?
- ☐ try to stop you from ordinary socializing with friends, visiting your family, or talking with members of the other sex?
- ☐ use threats to make you do what she wants? (This could include bribery or threats to withhold affection or to hurt herself.)
- ☐ make you feel you deserve to be punished or abused?
- ☐ isolate you from people who really care about you?
- ☐ get so upset when you express a different opinion that you always give in, just to keep peace?

If you said yes to even one of the preceding questions, you may be in an abusive relationship and need to get help. If you do nothing, things will almost surely get worse. Do not think that marriage to such a person would help her or make the relationship better. God's design is for marriage to be a relationship of respect and love, not one of dependence and fear. Abuse is not only physical, but includes emotional abuse, verbal abuse, and controlling behavior. If you or a friend is being abused, look for a safe way to show that it won't be tolerated. Look to parents or a trusted adult for help.

You can also look to other trusted adults for examples of what healthy relationships look like. Perhaps you know couples who have been married for a long time. They may welcome the chance to talk with you about their marriage. The Bible's description of love teaches us about Christ, but it also teaches us about the attitudes and behaviors between husband and wife. The entire life of a Christian will reflect both sorrow for when we fail to love one another and perseverance in prayerful hope that the Holy Spirit will continue to strengthen us in love toward one another.

"Love is patient and kind; love does not envy or boast; it is not arrogant or rude. It does not insist on its own way; it is not irritable or resentful; it does not rejoice at wrongdoing, but rejoices with the truth. Love bears all things, believes all things, hopes all things, endures all things" (1 Corinthians 13:4–7).

Relationships

Once you begin to date a young woman and the two of you spend more time together, you will begin to experience the joys and frustrations of being in a relationship. A dating relationship does have some level of commitment and expectation. It is not marriage, nor should you or your girlfriend expect all of the benefits and challenges of marriage: sexual intimacy, financial responsibility, total emotional vulnerability, and complete devotion to the other's needs. In dating, there are still limits and boundaries. This is God's design for you and your girlfriend. You should continue to ask yourself and each other if marriage is part of your future together. If not, perhaps stepping back from the relationship is in order. The risk of deep emotional hurt at breaking up and the temptation to increased sexual intimacy without the security of marriage will only increase if marriage is out of the picture for the two of you. Following are some additional scenarios that may help you evaluate if this relationship is headed for heartbreak or for the lifelong commitment of marriage.

Scenario 1: Right now my girlfriend and I (both seventeen years old) think we want to spend the rest of our lives together. Since we realize we'll both change a lot in the next few years, how can we keep from getting too serious too soon?

Each of you should have some activities in which you are independent of the other—different jobs, schools, clubs; this will help you learn to know yourselves as individuals. Talk honestly and openly about what is happening in your relationship. Make individual plans for the future, and remind yourselves that joint plans must be tentative. Talk about God's design for marriage and sexuality and how you can honor sexual purity in your relationship. Together, ask Him to help you guard against hurting each other with too much physical intimacy too soon.

If the two of you change and decide to break up, you will be able to do so without shame and possibly remain friends. It is good to look back on a relationship and cherish the things you learned, how you served your girlfriend, and how you were able to keep your sexual purity intact for your future wife.

Scenario 2: I can't help being very jealous of my girlfriend. One day, a note fell out of her pocket. I grabbed it and read it. It was from another boy! It was just about their history assignment, but I was furious! Shouldn't she stop exchanging notes with other boys when she's my girlfriend?

Do the words "my girlfriend" mean a close, caring relationship, or do they mean owning another person? Very few people are willing to have no life at all outside a relationship. Even in marriage, most people do not read their spouse's mail unless invited to do so.

Relationships you have now teach you about the characteristics and values that are important to a marriage by God's design. Trust is one of these characteristics. You will trust your wife to love and care for you when you look your best and when you don't, when you are happy and when you are not, when you can take care of yourself and when you need help. Marriage brings the secure feeling that no matter what, your wife is there for you, and only you. It is important to trust your girlfriend now unless she has given you reason to not trust her.

Talk with your girlfriend to get a better understanding of how she views friendships with other young men. Does she think it is okay to flirt with them even while you are dating? Does she include you when making plans that involve other young men? Her answers to these types of questions will help you determine if your girlfriend considers the two of you to be on the path to marriage. If not, it is okay to step away and end the dating relationship.

Scenario 3: I have been offered a summer job at a camp about 150 miles from home. My girlfriend has a good job right here in town. If I go away, we might not see each other all summer. I need the money and the experience, but is it worth taking a chance on losing my girlfriend?

By the time fall comes, both of you will be more independent, more interesting people. You'll have many new experiences and ideas to share. You could end up closer than ever.

Even if you stay at home, your relationship may end. Dating is about learning about the other person and determining if she shares your understanding of the service, sacrifice, and forgiveness that are required in a Christian marriage. Sometimes what is learned is that it is best to end the dating relationship. It hurts when a relationship ends, but clinging to a girlfriend now and believing that one single event in your life could end it is probably an indication that you both need to mature a bit more. Big decisions like the one you need to make should not be impacted by a fear of losing your girlfriend.

Scenario 4: I've been dating my girlfriend for about four months, but lately she's been talking about maybe getting married someday. Even though I like her a lot, I'm not ready to even think about being serious. I don't want to lose her, and I don't want to hurt her. What can I do?

Be honest with your girlfriend. Ask Jesus to help you speak honestly to her about how you view this relationship. The conversation could be painful, but it's not fair to let her believe you see the future as she does when you really do not.

But what will happen if you let things go on as they are? Steady dating at a young age can lead to marriage before one or both of you are ready. Five or ten years later, you may regret closing off your options at such a young age and you may want out. Of course, many young marriages do succeed. But statistics show that teenage marriages are three times as likely to fail as are marriages of people in their twenties. By shrinking from painful honesty now, you could store up a lot more pain for both of you—and for possible children—later.

Scenario 5: I like a girl now, but I feel like maybe I should keep searching for the perfect girl.

If you are praying to find the "right one" for you, remember to put your trust in God. God is in control, and He always has our best interests in mind. You have the Christian freedom to find a woman who shares your beliefs and values, who loves God and understands His design for marriage. There may be many women "out there" who will make a good wife for you. God did not make a "soul mate" for you. However, God promises to bless your marriage, and He will knit you together physically and emotionally. According to the Bible, when a man and a woman get married, it is God who joins them together (Mark 10:9).

Keep in mind, however, that because of the consequences of sin, you will struggle with challenges in your life and relationships. You will never find someone who always agrees with you and makes you perfectly happy. You will date sinners. If you marry, you will marry a sinner. Remember also that you are a sinner. But the forgiveness of Christ is for you—and for your future wife, if you marry. There is no such thing as "the right one" or someone who is "perfect" for you. Only Christ was perfect. Learn more about the young woman you like now and decide if she shares your love of Christ and your desire to serve others in the way God designed!

Scenario 6: I have been upset ever since my girlfriend broke up with me. I had no idea that breaking up would make me feel so bad.

The grief that you are feeling is a powerful emotion. You might also be feeling anger or frustration. It is very difficult for a young man to know what to do when a young woman ends the relationship. It hits right in the center of your pride.

Read the Bible, particularly Psalm 4, which begins: "Answer me when I call, O God of my righteousness!" You might recognize some of the frustration that the psalm writer (a man) includes in his prayer. Make David's prayer your prayer and talk to God, asking Him to help you recover from the anger and the hurt. You may not feel better at first, but He is listening and cares for you.

Remember that Jesus often works through other people. Find a trustworthy friend you can spend some time with just being a guy again. If possible, establish a friendly relationship with your former girlfriend. You can forgive her for the pain she caused you and you can apologize if anything you did contributed to the breakup. This is also a good time to get reacquainted with family, develop new interests, and enjoy time with other friends.

When you do begin dating again, be cautious for a while. Your pride has been hurt. Don't rush into a new relationship. You may unconsciously be using the new person to prove something to your former girlfriend.

Intimacy

With dating and relationships, you will be challenged to discover what types of physical intimacy are consistent with God's design for your sexuality. In a very real way, this may be the first time that the Christian beliefs and values you have learned since childhood are challenged. God's design for your sexuality is good and it benefits you and your future wife, but knowing this does not make the challenge to remain sexually pure and decent easy to meet. Resisting sin and selfish desires is never easy. Consider the following scenarios and how they might help you make decisions that are consistent with what you believe and confess about God's good design for sex. Then, pray for strength for you and your girlfriend to resist temptation and to develop a strong relationship of trust, love, and understanding that will help you both overcome the weakness of your flesh. You know God's will; pray for the strength to abide in it!

Scenario 1: How far can I go and still respect myself and my girlfriend?

Before anyone will respect you, you must respect yourself. Instead of asking "How far can I go?" consider what is best for you and your girlfriend as children of God. What honors God as the Creator of male and female?

God has reserved sexual intimacy for marriage. Sexual intercourse and other sexual acts are sexual intimacy. Perhaps it is most practical for you to let your conscience be the best gauge of how far you can go. Your conscience is a gift from God to help you curb sinful desires.

If you can kiss, hug, and hold your girlfriend and still keep your thoughts of her sexually pure, then that is a good guide for how far to go. If you begin to more aggressively kiss or hug her and your body starts to urge you to go further, then that is too far. Your conscience will be telling you it is time to stop, so listen.

God desires you to be different. He desires His people to be set apart—to not act like those who do not know and trust in Jesus as their Savior. "For the grace of God has appeared, bringing salvation for all people, training us . . . to live self-controlled, upright, and godly lives in the present age" (Titus 2:11–12).

Scenario 2: How can I tell how much intimacy I can have with a girl?

A good relationship is based on God's Word and includes respect, responsibility, and communication. The intimacy the two of you desire to share is something you should discuss with each other in light of God's Word. If you are not comfortable discussing intimacy and God's design for sex with each other, then can you really say you should take that next step of having sex?

If the two of you don't share an understanding about sexual purity, decency, and the gift of marriage, then it is time to step back and start discussing other fundamental things you believe about God. As a young Christian man, it is important for you to lead your relationship in a godly way. This is a discussion that you should begin with your girlfriend when the dating becomes a bit more serious. The Bible describes your role as husband as being the head, the leader, and the one who takes responsibility. As you learn about godly relationships, you are also learning about your role of leadership in marriage.

Once you discuss the limits of your intimacy, then honor the boundaries God established for you. Do not push your girlfriend to go farther, even if your body pushes you for more. Exercise self-control and respect. A young Christian man will have to do very tough things in his life as a Christian husband, father, and worker.

Scenario 3: I love my girlfriend very much, and I know she loves me, but I'm afraid of getting out of control. What can we do?

Avoid unsupervised and unplanned situations, as well as alcohol. Instead, focus on your love and respect for your girlfriend and for your relationship. Your mutual love for each other and for Jesus (who loves you both) makes all the difference. When you truly care for someone, you are not likely to put your own temporary pleasure ahead of the long-term happiness of both persons. When you believe in Jesus, His will and His love for you are the foundation of the relationship.

Remember that the farther you go along the road that leads to intercourse, the more difficult it is to put on the brakes and turn around. However, it is always possible to stop. You—and your faith in Jesus—are stronger than your physical desire.

As has been mentioned already, these situations may seem very trying for you, but they are real opportunities to practice and cultivate the traits necessary to become a godly man. By controlling yourself, you are letting your girlfriend know that you are willing to serve, cherish, and respect her. This self-control may be one of your most attractive qualities to a young woman also seeking to follow God's plan for her sexuality.

Scenario 4: My girlfriend says she loves me more than I love her because she's ready for intercourse and I'm not. I'm afraid I will lose her if I don't do what she wants.

It might be surprising that a girl is pressuring you for sex when you are willing to hold back. That certainly isn't the typical scenario. You should feel good that your faith in Jesus is shaping your decisions. You might try talking with her about your faith and the choices you make as a Christian man that will honor her and God. If your girlfriend is a Christian, you may be able to explore together what God's Word says about God's design for sex and about the beauty of sexual intercourse within the marriage relationship (see chapter 7).

If your girlfriend is not a Christian and remains insistent, ask yourself, what kind of love for you does she have if it requires you to disobey God in order to satisfy her physical desires? Is it lust masquerading as love? Do you want to encourage a continuing pattern where she uses pressure to get whatever she wants? If she's threatening to break up with you unless you do what she wants, is this the kind of love you can build a future on?

Jesus loves us more than anyone else does. And although He is also God, Jesus was a servant. He left His throne in heaven to come to earth to become human. He suffered and died so that our sins would be forgiven and we would be able to live together forever. Jesus did not look at what was in it for Himself. Love does things for others and is not self-serving. If your girlfriend loves and respects you, she will wait to have sex with you until marriage. She will recognize that this honors you and God. If she is still not willing to wait, then it is time for you to end the relationship.

Scenario 5: How can I get the willpower to say "This far and no farther" and stick to it? I feel so guilty sometimes, even though I have never had intercourse.

You need to talk to God about those guilty feelings. Remember, there is no sin so terrible that you cannot ask for—and receive—Christ's forgiveness. He will never, for any reason, stop loving you.

Whatever you've been doing that you feel guilty about, don't do it! Of course, that isn't as easy as it sounds, especially when willpower is something you feel you lack. You probably have the will, but not the power.

The good news is that the power to overcome temptation doesn't come from you. The power comes from Christ who died for you and rose again. He lives in you. The more your faith is strengthened by the Holy Spirit, the more you will rely on His power and not yours. So, read your Bible, pray, and commune with Him in His Supper. As you get ready to go out on a date, ask Him to be with you, and trust in His power, not your own.

The power He gives you is not a matter of gritting your teeth and being too serious. When things get intense on a date, often a little humor will relieve the tension. Or you can explain to your date, quite seriously, that you care too much about her to let anything happen you would both regret.

Scenario 6: Is sexting a safe alternative to having sex?

Sexting occurs when a male or female sends sexually explicit messages or images on a phone or other device. Popular culture would have us believe that sexting is a normal part of how men and women interact today. But this type of conversation is not God-pleasing.

Although the body is a wonderful gift of God to be admired, sexting degrades the body, treating it as a sexual object for personal gratification.

Sexting does not promote healthy conversation and communication. A relationship that centers around physical attraction and lust will not last and will only lead to emotional pain. Again, as with any sexual temptation, it is best to keep in mind what God's Word says, "Whatever is true . . . whatever is pure, whatever is lovely . . . think about these things" (Philippians 4:8).

Tell the person sexting you that you don't feel comfortable with the conversation and change the subject. If the person continues sexting, do not reply to the inappropriate texts, and block the caller.

Also be aware that sending nude or sexually explicit photos of someone younger than eighteen years old constitutes child pornography. Teens have been charged and convicted of this very serious crime.

Scenario 7: I'm not married, and I think I got a girl pregnant. What should I do? Where can I go for help? I can't tell my parents.

Right now you are probably feeling panicky, guilty, and worried. Maybe you think you have destroyed your relationship with your parents—or even your relationship with God. Are you wondering whether your parents will ever forgive you? Will God forgive you?

God will. Talk to Him about what you have done and how you feel. Jesus didn't scold the woman caught in the act of adultery. Instead, He protected her from those who would harm her and sent her home with the words "from now on sin no more" (John 8:11).

Jesus will forgive both you and the baby's mother—and He will gladly welcome you back. Remember the parable of the lost sheep (Luke 15:1–7). Jesus will stick by you in the difficult times ahead.

Remember, too, that God works through other people—your parents, for instance. If you feel unable to talk to your parents right now, you might try talking to

- a pastor or church youth worker;
- a school counselor or school nurse; or
- your family doctor or a doctor at a clinic.

Professional ethics forbid any of the professionals listed above from telling your parents without your consent (unless, of course, there is neglect or abuse involved, or a physical threat). These counselors care about you and want you to feel like you can be open and honest with them. Whoever you talk to probably will urge you to confide in your parents without delay. They won't talk to your parents themselves without first asking you, but they likely will suggest that it's in your best interests. Following are some good reasons to talk to your parents.

Your parents are likely to be more supportive, more helpful, more forgiving than you think. Yes, they may be angry and hurt at first, but they will be even more hurt when they find out later that you have shut them out of this crisis in your life.

They are almost certain to find out sooner or later. Even now, they are probably uneasily aware that something is wrong. When you lie to someone you love, you move farther and farther away from them. The secret makes a wall between you and people who love you.

You and your girlfriend will face some important decisions that will profoundly affect the lives of several people, including your unborn child. Help and support will be very important as you explore the consequences of each option open to you and as you think through the moral issues involved so that someday you can look back and say, "I made the right choice."

A caring, professionally trained Christian counselor can help you, your parents, and your baby's mother understand one another better. Even when parents try hard to forgive and understand, they can't easily get rid of their feelings of anger, disappointment, and failure. This will be a very painful time for all of you, and you need all the support you can get.

Through the entire situation, you need to be strengthened in your faith. Your parents can help provide resources for you, and worshiping together as a family will be a great source of strength. Your parents will pray for you and with you. Nothing will help more than God strengthening you through His Word.

Scenario 8: One of my friends is pregnant and not married. Should she keep her baby, give the baby up for adoption, or have an abortion?

Abortion ends a life that God has created, and it should not be considered as an option. Nonetheless, your friend and her family face a difficult time as they decide whether to keep the baby or allow the baby to be adopted by another family. This young mother must compare the love and care she is able to give her child with what adoptive parents can give.

These days, many unmarried mothers decide to keep their babies. Others choose to allow their babies to be adopted. If a mother decides to give her baby to an adoptive family, she is making a very difficult, heart-breaking decision, but this decision will bring joy to a couple who may have been waiting for years for a baby. Church-affiliated adoption agencies have long been placing babies in Christian homes.

The temptation to consider abortion is very great in today's culture. Sadly, in many states, free or low-cost clinics make it possible for teens to get abortions without the consent or knowledge of their parents. Many do not counsel that, medically speaking, abortion is an invasive medical procedure with many known complications. Abortion clinics are not regulated as strictly as hospitals, so there are greater risks when having an abortion done there, especially after the first three months of pregnancy.

In other words, your friend could make an irreversible decision without the support of people who love her very much. Abortion is not an easy or quick way of dealing with an unwanted pregnancy. Killing a preborn baby is not like having an infected tooth pulled. Your friend is dealing with a living human being, created by God just as she was created by God. Even those who do not believe in God may experience guilt, grief, and psychological and emotional scars after an abortion.

The consequences of an abortion—physical and emotional—are rarely discussed in the media or by pro-choice groups. If your friend is considering an abortion, encourage her to talk to her pastor, parents, and other trusted adults who value her life and the life of her baby.

Scenario 9: My girlfriend and I had sex, and now she's pregnant. What does the Bible say about abortion?

Just because our society allows abortions doesn't mean that it is okay. Our society has moved very far away from God's design for life. Twenty-two percent of all pregnancies end in abortion. Four in 10 unintended pregnancies end in abortion. In 2011, there were over 1 million abortions. This is a terrible sin!

There is no way to justify killing a human baby at whatever stage of life—even though some claim an abortion is justified if it saves the mother (and father) from embarrassment, broken plans for the future, or emotional pain. Only God has the right to give and take away life. Killing an **embryo** or **fetus** is killing a baby! He or she hasn't been born yet, but he or she is a human person.

We have already talked about God's design for marriage. When people don't follow God's design and have sex before marriage, they selfishly look to gratify their own desires. Sometimes there are natural consequences to this behavior.

Having an unintended pregnancy is life changing and will bring new challenges because you aren't prepared for parenthood. But killing the baby through abortion because you're not ready to be a parent is a selfish way to avoid responsibility. When you start to have sex, you need to be ready for the possibility of becoming a father. Half of all pregnancies among American women are unintended.

To know what the Bible says about abortion is to know what God says about babies in the womb. The Bible says that each of us has a special relationship with God that began before we were born. Jeremiah writes: "The word of the Lord came to me, saying, 'Before I formed you in the womb I knew you, before you were born I consecrated you; I appointed you a prophet to the nations'" (Jeremiah 1:4–5).

God formed Jeremiah in the womb and knew Jeremiah before he was born. God set Jeremiah apart for service and appointed work for him to do as an adult.

David, the psalm writer and king, is even more specific about God's role in creating life in the **womb**: "You [God] formed my inward parts; You knitted me together in my mother's womb. . . . My frame was not hidden from You, when I was being made in secret. . . . Your eyes saw my unformed substance; in Your book were written, every one of them, the days that were formed for me, when as yet there was none of them" (Psalm 139:13–16).

God created and knew David before he was born. He gave David all the days of his life.

If God created and knew both Jeremiah and David, He certainly created and knows you—and your unborn baby. He has the number of your days (your life) all known to Him and has good works set aside for you to do.

The Bible also emphasizes the value of each human life. "You shall not murder" (Exodus 20:13) is one of the Ten Commandments God wrote with His own hand and gave to His people. Why? Because God is good, all that He creates is precious. No one ever has the right to murder another person.

God values all life. Life is so special that God sent His own Son to be born of a young human mother so that through His life, death, and resurrection, all people could be forgiven, share His love on earth, and have eternal life in heaven.

Scenario 10: But what if it's too late? My girlfriend was afraid and embarrassed and had an abortion.

Many Christians who have chosen abortion have later regretted it with all their heart. They need to hear over and over again that through Jesus there is complete forgiveness. The blood of Jesus cleanses us from all sin (1 John 1:7). If your girlfriend had an abortion and you knew about it, or even if you didn't know, you can trust that this sin, too, went to the cross with Jesus Christ. Your girlfriend's pain, your pain, and the consequences of sin may endure, but your guilt should not! Ponder these wonderful truths:

"If we confess our sins, He [Jesus] is faithful and just to forgive us our sins and to cleanse us from all unrighteousness" (1 John 1:9).

"He is the propitiation [atoning sacrifice] for our sins, and not for ours only but also for the sins of the whole world" (1 John 2:2).

"There is therefore now no condemnation for those who are in Christ Jesus. For the law of the Spirit of life has set you free in Christ Jesus from the law of sin and death. For God has done what the law, weakened by the flesh, could not do. By sending His own Son in the likeness of sinful flesh and for sin, He condemned sin in the flesh" (Romans 8:1–3).

So lay your burden on Christ. "As far as the east is from the west, so far does He remove our transgressions from us. As a father shows compassion to his children, so the LORD shows compassion to those who fear Him" (Psalm 103:12–13).

Scenario 11: My girlfriend and I dated for about two years. We thought we loved each other and sincerely intended to get married someday. After we broke up, I felt pretty guilty. Even though we never had intercourse, we came close to it many times. I've asked God to forgive me, and I know He has, but somehow I don't feel forgiven. Why do my guilty feelings keep coming back?

It is unlikely that the guilt you feel now will be a problem years later in your life. You acknowledged your sin and have been forgiven in Christ. In Christ, you are free. Satan does like to remind us of our past sins, but the forgiveness in Christ defeats Satan's old accusations. When you feel your conscience accusing you, say, "I am forgiven in Christ," and gladly go about your day.

The emotional recovery from a breakup remains a difficult thing. Be thankful to God that you learned more about how you behave in a relationship and about the qualities you value in a future wife. Allow yourself time to recover from the pain, guilt-free because you are forgiven, and wiser with a better understanding of the consequences of going too far or of making promises outside of marriage.

The other thing to remember is that it takes time—and usually some small mistakes—to fully develop a strong sense of self-control. That's why we often use the term *cultivate* when discussing how to build up godly qualities. The results don't appear overnight; they take time and constant weeding, watering, and nourishing with Bible study, going to church to receive His gifts, and prayer. Growing up in Christ is a daily process that extends over seasons of time. Having a goal to work toward is great, but realize that you have to practice before you will hit your mark consistently.

Finding Out If Love Is Real

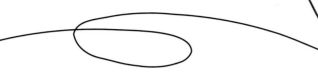

By God's Design Devotion

Read 1 Corinthians 13:1–8a.

"Love is patient and kind; love does not envy or boast" (1 Corinthians 13:4).

What examples have you seen of marriage? What do you expect marriage to be? Maybe you think of getting married and living a comfortable life with a nice house, a good job, and maybe a kid. Or maybe your picture is less rosy. Perhaps you have seen married people who constantly fight, say unkind things to and about each other, manipulate to get their way, or end their marriage in divorce. Both of these pictures of marriage are unsettling when you are still trying to discover what love in marriage looks like.

In God's design, there's more to marriage than nice things to own. Married people show patience and kindness toward each other; they don't focus on themselves or what they wish they had; they aren't rude to each other. They yield to each other's opinions when helpful; they don't resent their spouse's success; they forgive each other for mistakes. They remain faithful through hard times and never stop loving each other.

God's design for marriage reflects the love that He has for His Church. In marriage we have the chance to demonstrate God's love to another person for the rest of our lives. As you consider your future marriage relationship, remember that God wants you to have this mutually supportive relationship someday.

Prayer: Dear God, Your love endures all things and never ends. Thank You for demonstrating how much You love me by sending Jesus to suffer, die, and rise again for me. Please strengthen the woman I am going to marry, and give me patience to wait for her. In Jesus' name. Amen.

As you grow in your understanding of God's design for marriage and sexuality, you may find yourself in more serious relationships. You may be wondering how your faith in Jesus and your desire to live your life as a Christian man apply to the practical question of whether you have a love that will last a lifetime. In other words, "Is this the woman I might marry?"

What is the difference between infatuation and real love?

How can we tell if our love will last?

What qualities am I looking for in a wife?

What qualities are important to have in common with the woman I will marry?

What does it mean if we fight?

Will marriage change us?

Will our marriage last?

At sixteen years old, you are deeply in love with your girlfriend, and she feels the same way about you. You live for the times when you are together. It feels like you share a world of your own. You feel intense excitement and pleasure each time you touch or even see each other. Is your love only infatuation—"puppy love"? No. It is real and genuine. When you promise to love each other always, you both really mean it.

But will your love last? It might. Then again, it might not. At this point in your lives, there's no way to tell. Between the ages of 15 and 21, most people change interests, attitudes, and sometimes even values. People discover new talents within themselves. They observe the way others live their lives and make some decisions influenced by them. Decisions about jobs, colleges, where you want to live, going to church, and volunteering are some examples of choices that get influenced by other people you meet and respect in young adulthood.

Chances are you both will fall in love quite a few more times before you make a final choice of a spouse. Each time, you will learn more about how to love, how to serve, and how to be loved and served by your girlfriend. You both will reevaluate what is important. These are times to consciously ask what priority God has in your relationship and what part your faith in God has in shaping your decisions. Do the two of you together make godly decisions that obey Him and serve each other? Keeping God central will build your relationship on a solid foundation and increase your understanding of what it means to be male and female knitted together by God in mutual love and service.

If love is based mainly on physical attraction, it may not last long. Without mutual love and respect, sexual attraction withers away, sometimes quickly.

If you are wondering whether your love is temporary, notice the ways in which the relationship has changed you. If people say you have changed—and not for the better—look out! But if you are kinder, more responsible, more self-confident than you were before, you've got a good thing going, at least for this stage in your life. Remember that "for those who love God all things work together for good, for those who are called according to His purpose" (Romans 8:28). God often uses a good relationship with another person to bring out the best in those He loves.

What to Look for in Someone to Love

It may be tempting to put together a "wish list" for the perfect wife. No such list is possible, however. Instead, as a husband, you will make a vow to love, cherish, and honor your wife for the rest of your life, despite what changes she may experience physically, emotionally, or mentally.

Sin remains in our world and mars us. Accidents happen that change our physical abilities and appearance. Emotional and mental challenges and assaults change a person's personality and attitudes. The person you marry when you are young is not likely to be the same person as the two of you grow old together.

The vow you make in marriage and the commitment you make to your wife is blessed by God. By His mercy and grace, you will be blessed with the ability to love your wife, regardless of what changes may come. The love between husband and wife is not based on character traits or qualities. It is based on the commitment to love and serve until death separates you.

With that understanding of marital love and commitment, does that mean you can choose any random person as a spouse and all will be well? No. It remains important to think deeply and pray about the qualities the Bible says make a good husband and a good wife. Then, as you get to know different people, you will discover the blessings and gifts given to them. You will be attracted to qualities and traits that may be similar to your own, that complement yours, or that are totally different from yours.

Ready to Serve as a Man of God

"He has told you, O man, what is good; and what does the Lord require of you but to do justice, and to love kindness, and to walk humbly with your God?" (Micah 6:8).

Do you live your faith? Are you someone who is dependable, whose word can be trusted? Are you able to laugh at yourself, able to see the funny side of life? Do you make an effort to be considerate, to treat people as you would like to be treated? Do you try to see things from the other person's point of view?

Micah 6:8 describes the characteristics of a good man. He does what the Lord requires of him. He upholds justice in the treatment of others. He loves kindness and walks humbly with God. All these characteristics show humility and service to God and to others. They are easy words to remember, but difficult to do on your own. Ask God for help to be this humble servant.

You don't need to rush to marriage. Allow yourself time to mature. You may tire of being a man alone, like Adam. It may seem like love or marriage will never come. But God blesses you with these things in His time. You can't make them happen. Be patient and serve others while you "wait in the LORD; be strong, and let your heart take courage; wait for the Lord!" (Psalm 27:14).

While you wait, here are some love signs you can watch for, some ways to test the durability of your love once you are blessed with a serious relationship with a young woman.

The truest, best sign of love is what has been modeled by Christ. His unconditional, self-sacrificing love is the best model of love. Jesus was willing to give His life for us on the cross; He took our hurt upon Himself so that we would not be separated from Him forever . . . and instead, so that we would *live* with Him forever (1 Peter 2:24)!

The Bible gives a picture of what your relationship with your spouse should be like, when the time comes. Jesus is the Groom, and the Church (all Christians) is the Bride. A husband's love is to be self-sacrificial. A man is willing to sacrifice his own wants and desires for his wife and to think of his wife's needs before his own. A wife honors and respects her husband as the Church honors Jesus. God promised the Church that He would never leave her. A husband is to remain faithful to his wife his whole life. Marriage brings with it such a special companionship and trust.

Through God's Word, Jesus empowers His followers to "walk in love, as Christ loved us and gave Himself up for us, a fragrant offering and sacrifice to God" (Ephesians 5:2). Jesus has promised to "equip you with everything good that you may do His will, working in us that which is pleasing in His sight, through Jesus Christ" (Hebrews 13:21). He strengthens you to love!

What Do We Have in Common?

Love shares the same Christian faith in Jesus as Savior from sin, and it shares the same values of service toward each other. Although you may have to compromise on differences about day-to-day activities, you should not compromise on your beliefs and what you know is true based on God's Word.

However, your future wife may be different from you in many other ways. Is that okay? Most of us would say we want an intelligent spouse. But what we probably mean is that we'd like someone who is about as intelligent as we are, someone who has had about the same amount of education. When two people of unequal intelligence try to discuss anything, they both may feel bored and frustrated.

The same thing is true of many other qualities. To one person, *adventurous* might mean a willingness to try a new restaurant (provided a friend recommends the place). To another person, *adventurous* might mean a spur-of-the-moment decision to move to Montana with no job, no money, and three children. There's nothing wrong with either of those attitudes, but those two people surely will have things to work through if they marry.

Often couples are attracted to each other by their differences. If you are a quiet, shy person, you might enjoy going out with an outgoing woman to help overcome your shyness. Be cautious, though. What often happens is that the quiet one is dragged to parties by the social one, or the social one sits unhappily at home with the quiet one.

Another common difference is family background. What will happen if these two people fall in love? His family life is lively, warm, and loud. He is the only one in his family who has graduated from high school. His parents value hospitality and always have an extra bed open for unexpected visitors. Her home, on the other hand, was always a quiet and restful place. Both of her parents have interesting, demanding careers, and they value education and travel. These differences in background could strengthen them as a couple, but it could also be a source of conflict.

Finally, your family and friends may recognize the compatibility found within a healthy dating relationship and share with you their approval. Don't underestimate the value of having your parents like your girlfriend or of being accepted by your girlfriend's family. That, too, is a part of how God knits us together within our families.

Will Marriage Change Us?

Yes. By God's design for marriage, as a husband, you will constantly learn more about your wife. You will also become better at serving each other and putting the other first. This will change you. Your whole attitude of selfishness becomes one of selflessness in a God-designed, Christian marriage. This is one of the most beautiful things about marriage.

You will also learn how every day you need to be forgiven by your wife and how to forgive her. Starting every day with the freshness of being forgiven creates a trust between husband and wife that cannot be found in any other relationship you have, even when you have a child.

How will this happen?

God's Holy Spirit enables Christians to grow in all the qualities that make a marriage a place of mutual love, respect, and service. The Holy Spirit blesses your marriage with "love, joy, peace, patience, kindness, goodness, faithfulness, gentleness, [and] self-control" (Galatians 5:22–23).

As you grow in your knowledge and faith in Christ, you will continue to learn how "love is patient and kind; love does not envy or boast; it is not arrogant or rude. It does not insist on its own way; it is not irritable or resentful; it does not rejoice at wrongdoing, but rejoices with the truth. Love bears all things, believes all things, hopes all things, endures all things. Love never ends" (1 Corinthians 13:4–8a).

Communication

In the best marriages, communication begins long before the couple heads for the church. Many hours need to be spent building your friendship, talking about

your faith in Christ;

your complete life histories;

your feelings about yourselves and your families; and

your interests, your sexuality, and your goals.

Along with sharing life histories and future plans, communication involves active, loving listening to everyday problems and feelings.

As your friendship becomes stronger, you both will be better at listening without being defensive or trying to justify yourself. Healthy communication isn't a matter of who is right or wrong; it is effectively conveying thoughts, emotions, or feelings in a way that is mutually understood. Sometimes it's far more important to be loving than to be right.

Compassionate listening can be difficult. Keep in mind that men and women often look at things from a different perspective. Men tend to try to fix problems. If their wife or girlfriend comes to them with a problem, they offer suggestions or assistance to fix it. Women don't always think the same way. Often a woman simply wants to express her frustrations to someone who loves her. She doesn't necessarily want a solution; she wants affirmation.

Many women rank "good listener" as one of the most important qualities in a man. Women tend to be very verbal and want to know they are with someone who can hear what is important to them. Keep in mind that all people are not equally verbal, but everyone can work at being a good listener.

Love cares about what the other person is thinking and feeling, and it is not just focused on one's own interests or topics of discussion. Love takes the time to explain things that are important and to listen to what the other person thinks is important. Remember that men and women communicate and listen in different ways, and both need forgiveness when things were assumed or misunderstood.

What Happens When We Fight?

People who love each other still do have disagreements, just like anybody else, but they have learned how to have disagreements while remaining close.

Some couples are afraid to talk honestly. "If I tell her about that, she'll be angry." "If I tell him what I've decided to do, he'll try to stop me." Each tells the other only what he or she wants to hear. Each is very careful to cover up problems before they cause any unpleasantness.

The problem here is dishonesty. God created us for deep communion with another. We cannot achieve this when we hide parts of ourselves from others out of fear. Remember that "there is no fear in love, but perfect love casts out fear" (1 John 4:18). It may be difficult, but in God's timing, each of us can work toward complete honesty in all parts of our relationships—even when we think our revelation may be unsettling.

If we don't develop this type of honesty, then when a disagreement does surface, each person may be surprised and hurt by the other's "unreasonable" anger, and terrible, wounding things might be said by both persons.

Talking through a disagreement is a lot easier than letting it get to the point where it becomes a big argument that tears you apart. As Christians, you can trust each other not to intentionally hurt each other. You also can offer forgiveness to each other when you slip and say or do something that hurts.

When disagreements and conflicts are resolved in forgiveness and understanding, your intimacy with your wife is strengthened. You will become a little closer each time you settle a problem in a way both can live with.

There are several ways to deal with conflict. For example, one person may sacrifice for the other:

Him: *Let's go to the movies tonight.*

Her: *I really had my heart set on staying home, but if it's important to you to go out tonight, I'll go.*

Or it may be possible to work out a compromise that meets both people's needs:

Him: *Let's go to the movies tonight.*

Her: *I really had my heart set on staying home, but if it's important to you to go out tonight, I'll go.*

Him: *Well, if you want to stay home, maybe together we can watch a movie on TV.*

Her: *That sounds like a good idea.*

Sometimes you will not be able to agree on certain issues. That can be a real test of your love and trust for each other. It's a time to say, "I love you even if I don't agree with you." If you can practice this kind of acceptance with people around you, it will be a lot easier to do in your marriage. You don't always have to agree about everything.

Of course, if the issue involves a matter of right and wrong or a clear command of God, you will want to keep on encouraging your wife to place God's command first. You will want to pray for strength and be devoted to studying God's Word to help you and your wife understand God's definition of Christian living.

Can We Talk to Each Other with Complete Honesty?

One of the joys of a good relationship is having someone to talk to. The more you feel comfortable sharing yourself with another person, the closer you will feel toward that person. All of us are at different levels, though, when it comes to what we think is complete honesty. You may want to share your innermost thoughts. The other person may have to think through an issue before sharing it with anybody. Do not pretend to be what you're not. In a good relationship, you are free to share your viewpoint, goals, and dreams without feeling ashamed or embarrassed. You can share your past with no risk of judgment.

A sign of love is complete trust in the other person. You are not afraid to be vulnerable and show the other person your true self.

This complete trust in another person is one of the joys of a strong relationship. It means not only trusting that you can be yourself with the other person and still be loved, but also trusting each other's faithfulness to the other. Where there is doubt or uncertainty of faithfulness to the relationship, there is a weakening of the relationship. If the person you're dating seriously has been unfaithful with another man while in a relationship with you, it will be difficult to judge the sincerity of her future loyalty and faithfulness to you. Love is not jealous or suspicious but rather full of peace and contentment. Honesty and trust go hand in hand. What a joy there is when we follow God's plan for relationships!

What about Our Faith? What If We Believe Different Things? What If We Belong to Different Churches?

A sign of love is a relationship centered on Christ. As you study God's Word, worship, and pray together, your faith is nurtured and strengthened. Having a Christ-centered relationship also means that the activities you do together are pleasing to God. Your relationship will be physically, emotionally, and spiritually healthy.

Can a marriage work if you and your spouse practice different religions? Yes, but it's not easy. The ideal is to share a belief in Christ and to belong to the same church so that you can share the practice of your faith completely. Christ should be the cornerstone of all relationships—certainly of a marriage. It is unfortunate when one or the other cannot share Him because of differences in belief or church practices. If you believe different things about Baptism, how will you handle the Baptism of your child? If you believe different things about God's Word, how will you grow spiritually together?

Another challenge with dating someone who doesn't share your same beliefs is that she may have a hard time understanding your desire to abstain from premarital sex. When a woman really loves you, she will know God's design for sex is the best thing for both of you and for any children born to you.

Remember that if you want a Christian marriage, marry a Christian. A marriage that is built on faith and trust in God is like no other relationship. When both husband and wife seek God's will in their lives, they are not alone in their struggle to make their marriage work. Their shared trust in God is the basis for all goals, values, and decisions. God provides them with the strength they need when trouble comes; He blesses them with a life together that is filled with forgiveness and joy.

Isn't There a 50 Percent Divorce Rate?

In a given year, you can compare the number of marriages to the number of divorces based on census data. For example, if you compare the 2011 divorce rate to the marriage rate based on Centers for Disease Control and Prevention (CDC) statistics, it looks like 53 percent! But consider how the increase of couples living together can lower the marriage rate. When fewer people are getting married, each divorce has a bigger impact on the divorce rate.

Here is a bit of hopeful news! One study, which tracked specific marriages over time, showed that approximately 43 percent of marriages (that took place among couples aged 15–46) ended in divorce. That is significantly lower that 53 percent! The study also found that divorce rates are higher if the marriage is a second or third marriage, if the marriage begins at an earlier age, or if the couple's level of education was a high school diploma or less. Many factors contribute to this 43 percent.

The study also reported more encouraging news for those young people who wait until after college to get married. At the fifteenth anniversary of marriages that were studied, 75 percent of those married couples were still married. Perhaps the trends in the divorce rate aren't so sad after all. You can have additional hope because other studies have shown that marriages where religious commitment is evident have a 35 percent lower divorce rate than nonreligious couples. Sharing faith in Jesus with your spouse is a crucial factor in resolving differences with forgiveness, sharing values, and honoring the vows made before God in your marriage.

And the divorce rate seems to be continuing its decline. Divorce rates peaked in 1981. Of the marriages that began after that, the number that have ended was lower when compared with the marriages that began in the 1970s.

Don't let statistics scare you out of getting married because you think you might only have a fifty-fifty chance of staying together! A survey for family growth conducted by the CDC showed that, compared with unmarried people, married men and women tend to live longer, engage in fewer risky behaviors, take better care of their physical health, have increased sexual intimacy, make more money, and have more financial savings. All of these benefits are blessings from God.

As we've been saying, God has made us to be in relationships. We are healthiest when God and others are a part of our lives. We were not made to be alone. Even if it's not God's will for us to get married, we are still intimately connected with our brothers and sisters in the family of God. We are also sinful people, so our relationships won't be free from conflict; but through Christ in us, our relationships can be full of love, forgiveness, and reconciliation. All these relationships can be encouraging, fulfilling, and rewarding by God's design.

Marriage: When Two Become One

By God's Design Devotion

Read Ecclesiastes 4:9–12.

"A threefold cord is not quickly broken" (Ecclesiastes 4:12).

Think of a braid formed by three strands twisted together. If there were only two strands, they could easily become unraveled. There is nothing keeping them together. When you have a third strand in the braid, it keeps the other two connected.

The Bible uses this metaphor to talk about human relationships, and it is often applied to marriage. If you get married, you and your wife will be bound together like two strands. God is the third strand; without Him, your relationship will have nothing to keep it together. If you are both connected to the love of God through hearing His Word, your marriage will be strengthened and you will be even more closely connected to each other.

May your future marriage always keep God at the center, binding your lives together.

> **Prayer: God, thank You for the gift of marriage that allows Your children to draw close to each other and to You. Thank You for setting me free from the bonds of the devil through Jesus' death and resurrection. In Jesus' name I pray. Amen.**

This is the part you are waiting for, right? By God's design, you have valued and honored His gift of sexuality. You have struggled to exercise self-control. Now you bring sexual purity to your soon-to-be wife. If you have failed in that sexual purity, rejoice now that you are forgiven in Christ; then confess this sin to your fiancée and receive her forgiveness also. Then, prepare for the beautiful gift of sexuality that God designed for you to share together.

Think back to the creation story you read in the beginning of this book. When God created the first man and woman, He blessed them and joined them together in a one-flesh union. He commanded them to multiply. They were male and female, uniquely created to fit together, to be knitted together emotionally and physically, in shared communion with each other and with God. Since the fall into sin, there are still challenges, but sexuality within marriage is far more powerful and wonderful than most people imagine! It is the pinnacle of the one-flesh union! And now, we will talk about this wonderful gift you will share with your wife.

What actually happens in sexual intercourse?

What difference does marriage make in a sexual relationship?

How often does a married couple have intercourse?

Is there a secret to a happy marriage?

What Happens in Sexual Intercourse?

Sexual intercourse is more than a physical act. When God says that a man and woman become one flesh, it means they share all things in the most deep and intimate ways. Emotions, thoughts, desires, hopes, dreams—all are shared in the marriage. The Bible put it this way: "Did [the Lord] not make them one, with a portion of the Spirit in their union?" (Malachi 2:15).

When a married couple comes together intimately, there is a time before intercourse when the couple may touch, gently massage, and kiss each other. Ideally, they have talked about what types of physical touch they welcome and enjoy. The intimacy shared by husband and wife is without shame; it is open and mutually pleasurable. As the couple becomes more and more excited, heart rate and blood pressure go up dramatically. Muscles tense. In some people, a measles-like flush covers part of the body. The hormones and chemicals in the body are triggered to prepare for this intimate act.

Blood rushes into the man's penis and stays there, making it erect and hard. The woman's vagina expands and produces a lubricating fluid that makes intercourse easier. The muscles at the entrance to the vagina relax. Her clitoris enlarges at first, flattens out, and then seems to disappear under the fold of skin that ordinarily covers most of it.

When both husband and wife are ready, they work together to bring their bodies together, male and female, in the way that God designed. This creates a pleasurable feeling for both the husband and the wife. The brain is also involved, producing neurochemicals that heighten the emotions, increase the adrenaline, and stimulate nerve endings throughout the body.

Their excitement may build until one or both of them experience orgasm. The man's penis ejaculates semen; the woman's vagina contracts and expands several times; they may tremble with intense physical and emotional pleasure. Within the intimacy of marriage, this nakedness and pleasure can be shared without shame.

Then, all of the signs of arousal go away. A feeling of well-being and complete relaxation floods their bodies, also the result of a powerful brain chemical. This can be a special time of tenderness when they can lie in each other's arms, caressing and talking.

There may also be relief and peace that comes from the security of the marriage relationship. The couple can rest assured that the promises to love, honor, and cherish are in place, making it safe to be so vulnerable during intercourse, in complete nakedness, and as close to another human being as is possible. In marriage, such times of intimacy affirm the bonds of love.

Is Sex Always Like That?

No. Different couples have different needs, levels of comfort, and interest in this level of physical intimacy. There are many ways to share physical intimacy within marriage. Everyday affection and open communication strengthen the intimacy shared at these intensely physical times of lovemaking. As you become familiar with each other and talk with each other, you will find the many expressions of your love for each other that will bring mutual pleasure.

People have described intercourse as thrilling, soul-stirring, boring, shocking, deeply satisfying, painful, wonderfully comfortable, humiliating, confidence-building, disappointing, fascinating, disgusting, and delightful.

How can the same experience be so different for different people? God intends intercourse to be a superbly joyous way to express mutual love between a man and a woman in their marriage. In many different places, the Bible speaks very positively of sexual intercourse—always within marriage. (Different words are used to describe sex outside of marriage.) Does this mean that sex within marriage always feels wonderful and sex outside of marriage always feels terrible?

It isn't quite that simple. Researchers are finding that sex without commitment tends to be flat and joyless compared with sex within a marriage where trust, honesty, and caring are abundantly shared. But marriage alone does not do it. More is necessary.

What Things Make a Difference in Sexual Pleasure?

The couple's total relationship controls their ability to give and receive sexual pleasure. Before intercourse can be the great experience it is meant to be, couples need to have complete trust and confidence in each other. They need to know that they are loved unconditionally. With this type of love, each is free to suggest having intercourse, and each can say "Some other time" without the other feeling rejected.

If an unmarried man and woman try to use intercourse to become closer to each other, they will be disappointed. In marital intercourse, a couple celebrates their unity, the fact that their marriage makes them one flesh. Apart from marriage, this same activity can produce doubt and insecurity because two unmarried people have no such safety and security with each other. In a sense, rather than strengthen their bond, they weaken it because they have told lies with their bodies. They leave the bed to go live separate, uncommitted lives rather than a life joined together.

Even within a good relationship, the quality and intensity of a sexual experience varies greatly from one time to another. The pair will sometimes come to orgasm together, sometimes separately. Sometimes, one person will enjoy intercourse but will not come to orgasm at all.

For most people, the most important part of a sexual relationship is emotional intimacy. Their deepest needs are met by tenderness, closeness, and sharing. This is why the Book of Malachi talks about the union of flesh and spirit. This depth of emotional intimacy can only happen in a committed marriage because it happens by God's good design.

Love . . . "Till Death Do Us Part"

Once married, a husband and wife do not demand instant satisfaction of all personal desires. A spouse who is self-serving creates a challenge in the relationship because marriage is about serving the other. A marriage needs both spouses' energy and attention in order for it to stay strong and to grow. A marriage requires work *every day*! As a man and woman make their marriage vows, they should consider what promises about love they are really making:

- We will always listen to each other. We will call on God's power to work within us as we try to understand and meet the other's needs.
- Daily, we'll tell and show each other that "you are the most important person in my life." Secure in each other's love, we will not allow lesser relationships to threaten us.
- Because we recognize that all talents and successes are gifts from God, neither of us needs to "win," to be the most important one in the world's eyes.
- We will give each other the same politeness, consideration, and attention we give to a most honored guest.
- For each of us, the other's needs will be as important as our own. Recognizing that irritability is often caused by suppressed anger or worry, we will try to be open with each other about how we really feel. Because we care about each other, we will control words and actions that might hurt the other.
- Sometimes we will fail; sometimes we will hurt each other. But as forgiven sinners, we can forgive those wrongs without getting even and without keeping score.
- Because Christ lives in us, we can encourage each other to study His Word and live in His truth.
- We give total, lifelong commitment to this marriage and to each other. Even if bad times come, we will not give up; we will struggle, pray, love, and grow.
- We are one in Christ—until death do us part.

In 1 Corinthians 13:4–8, the qualities of biblical masculinity and femininity are displayed. Focused on Christ, a husband and wife can begin to love others as He loves us. This love is quick to apologize for failures and does not keep a record of a spouse's mistakes. The humility of self-giving love frees a spouse to love the other in the same way.

As you mature into adulthood, consider keeping these verses handy. They describe the type of love we are to show all others, not just our spouse. So whether you marry or remain single, the love of Christ in you that is patient and kind, not envious or boastful, is the love that serves others.

What Difference Does Marriage Make in a Sexual Relationship?

The marriage certificate is evidence of a public commitment to make the marriage work, "for better or for worse." You say to each other, "No matter what happens—physical changes or illnesses, emotional or mental struggles, spiritual challenges—I will be there. We bear all our struggles and blessings together." All of the people at a wedding witness the couple's promise to each other and can lovingly hold them accountable to their vows.

Another reason weddings have witnesses—often a church full of them—is that the health of each individual marriage also impacts the health of the community. If you reject your marriage vows, you hurt more than just your spouse. You weaken the entire community, which often has to work very hard to mitigate the damage of a failed marriage. One study found that just one divorce costs the state as much as $30,000, based on such things as the higher use of food stamps and public housing. The emotional and spiritual costs are even higher.

Some people are afraid of marriage since it means total commitment and total vulnerability. If you choose unwisely, you will be badly hurt. Some people have been hurt in the past and may have difficulty completely trusting someone. But if spouses hold back a little, afraid to risk too much of themselves, complete intimacy will not happen—emotionally or sexually. Outside the security of a lifetime commitment, any problem triggers anxiety, and the anxiety itself can be a barrier to mutual sexual fulfillment.

God intends that a man and a woman will "become one flesh" (Genesis 2:24) in marriage. The feelings of oneness in sexual intercourse do not necessarily happen overnight. Sometimes years of loving communication and continual adjustment are needed to reach a completely satisfying sexual relationship.

How Often Does a Married Couple Have Intercourse?

There are such wide differences among individuals that it is impossible to come up with a definition of what is "normal." Even for the same person, sexual desire will vary. Much depends on how one feels on a given day. As years go by, urgent physical needs often give way to the desire for a more complete emotional connection, but less frequent sexual experience. Most couples will continue to value sexual intercourse throughout their marriage. In fact, most people are physically capable of sexual activity until death.

While it is common for young newlyweds to focus on frequency of intercourse, especially if they have saved sexual relations for marriage, the more important question is whether each time of intimacy is marked by self-giving love. Some people mistakenly believe having lots of sex in marriage is the key to happiness, but troubles will surely arise if either spouse is simply using the other for his or her own sexual pleasure. If we are to view marital love in light of Christ's relationship to the Church, we know that sexual intimacy in marriage is about faithfully giving yourself to your spouse and knowing that your wife faithfully gives herself to you.

Is There a Secret to a Happy Marriage?

Build your marriage on Christ, on His forgiveness and love for each of you, and then it will not crumble when trouble comes. Jesus promised that "where two or three are gathered in My name, there am I among them" (Matthew 18:20). This is true in any group of Christians, but think of the power His promise adds to the intimate relationship of marriage! God works in and through husband and wife, helping each to share their love, "that your joy may be full" (John 15:11).

St. Paul compares Christian marriage to Christ's relationship with us, His Church (Ephesians 5:21–33). Christ's love is the model for the love we are to have toward our spouse: love that gives itself away, love that

© iStock.com / Andrew Rich

does not depend on the other doing anything or being anything, love that is totally without strings, love that does not have to be earned in any way.

People today still expect marriage to be a loving, deeply intimate joining of two people. This can be demanding as well as incredibly rewarding. Husbands and wives need to work together to resolve conflicts and to discuss disagreements with forgiveness and respect. They need to pray together for good communication. And they must work together to make a home and family for themselves. They will discuss:

How will we make sure God is the foundation of our home? What will we do to serve and praise Him?

What about God's gift of children? Do we envision a large family, a small one, or no children at all? Why? How will we approach childcare?

How will we handle our money? How will we decide what we can afford? What if we disagree?

How will we divide household tasks? Will we do it the way our parents did or will we develop our own patterns?

Where will we live? Will we both have careers outside our home? How will we share in leisure activities? What material things (house, cars, etc.) do we want?

Once you have discussed your family's needs and wants, you will need to decide how you and your wife can best meet these needs. Some things you desire or want may be sacrificed or postponed in order to satisfy your family's needs. Large homes, expensive vacations, new cars—these types of things are sometimes set aside in order to live within the financial means you have been given through your employment. If God blesses you with children, your family's needs change dramatically. As father and husband, you have the profound and rewarding responsibility to lead your family through these changes.

Things will change; only God's promises remain the same. He will help you handle all that comes your way. Being married isn't always a happy state because you are—and are married to—a sinner. However, through the grace of God, there is much peace and contentment in a marriage that is built on the love and forgiveness of Christ.

When Two Become Three

By God's Design Devotion

Read Ephesians 6:1–4.

"Fathers, do not provoke your children to anger, but bring them up in the discipline and instruction of the Lord" (Ephesians 6:4).

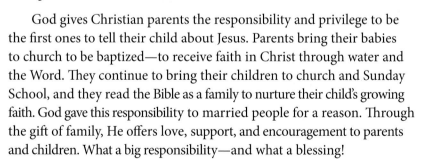

Becoming a parent is a huge responsibility! Babies need constant attention—they need to be fed in the middle of the night and have their diapers changed regularly. They also need to know they are safe and loved. In addition to his or her physical health, you also will care for your child's emotional and spiritual health.

God gives Christian parents the responsibility and privilege to be the first ones to tell their child about Jesus. Parents bring their babies to church to be baptized—to receive faith in Christ through water and the Word. They continue to bring their children to church and Sunday School, and they read the Bible as a family to nurture their child's growing faith. God gave this responsibility to married people for a reason. Through the gift of family, He offers love, support, and encouragement to parents and children. What a big responsibility—and what a blessing!

Prayer: Dear Jesus, thank You for dying on the cross and rising on Easter to pay for all of my sins. Thank You for my family and for giving me opportunities to love and serve those I live with. As I begin to consider getting married and becoming a parent, strengthen me and my future wife in love for You and for each other. In Your name. Amen.

As you mature and grow into a man after humbly walking in the way of God, you will find that marriage provides ample opportunities to become more Christlike. A person once called marriage "God's training ground for love." How beautiful and fulfilling it is to willingly give of yourself for another person! If this is true for marriage, how much more so when a person becomes a parent! The daily effort to care for and nurture children is full of rewards and challenges like few other experiences in life.

You may feel that you aren't ready to be a parent and may never be ready for such an awesome responsibility. You may wonder if you even want children. Wouldn't it be more fun to just be married without kids?

Think back again to the creation account in Genesis. God's first blessing to the new man and woman was that they "be fruitful and multiply and fill the earth" (Genesis 1:28). This wasn't a curse or a burden, although their sin led to struggle in all relationships involving people and pain in childbirth for the woman. Rather, God the Creator allowed humans to participate in His ongoing creation by bringing forth new living beings through their bodies fitting together. Remember Malachi 2:15: "Did [the Lord] not make them one, with a portion of the Spirit in their union? And what was the one God seeking? Godly offspring."

While being married and becoming a parent may be the most rewarding experience of your life, it's not something most people can step into without preparation. This chapter aims to answer some common questions about what is involved when God blesses you and your wife with the gift of a child.

Are we ready for a baby?

The honest answer is that one can never be "ready" for a baby. There is little that you have experienced in your life that compares with the joys and challenges of being a parent. Trusting that God is the author of life, that He chooses when you are "ready," you can be confident that our faithful Lord will provide all that you need to "be ready" when He grants this gift to you.

There are things you can do to be ready. You and your wife can cultivate in yourselves and in your marriage the love, service, and self-sacrifice that provide the best foundation for welcoming children into the world. However, even if a person is still a "work in progress" (and doesn't this describe all of us?), having children isn't something to fear or avoid.

You and your wife can also be working continually to build security in your relationship, working through the financial, emotional, and spiritual commitment necessary to have a good marriage and to be good parents. Regular worship, daily Bible study and time together in prayer, open discussions of finances and purchases, mutual care and help in household chores, and open support and communication to deal with outside stress all are building blocks for a strong Christian family.

Many couples, however, find themselves surprised by the joy of pregnancy without having worked all this out perfectly. This time of preparation can be an incredible time of bonding (and challenges) as the couple works on these issues.

Ultimately, the best time is God's time. He remains the one who blesses the union of the husband and wife. God alone grants life according to His will and in His time in order that a child should be conceived through the sexual union. It is our duty to trust that God will provide for our needs and the needs of our children, despite our own fears about how we can make a family work or fit into our schedule. God has promised to be with us and strengthen us throughout life's challenges. His promise to hear our prayers and the strength we find in His Word give us hope and can help us face the future with confidence and peace.

What are some of the challenges of having children?

Children are delightful, loving, cuddly charmers. They also whine, have nightmares, fight with each other, and test your patience to the limit. God both blesses us and teaches us through our children. As we respond to our children's needs, we become wiser, more responsible, more patient, and more unselfish than we would have thought possible! With God's help, you will face the challenges of having children the same way you face all challenges—in humility, in service to Him and your children, and in need of forgiveness for when you fail. The good parent is the godly parent who seeks His help and wisdom.

Some people misuse the gift of a child to strengthen a shaky marriage. This is not the proper response to God's gift of sexuality or the birth of a child, and it can cause many problems for you, your wife, and your child. We must be careful not to turn anyone, especially babies, into objects. Life must be respected and revered at all stages, not used for manipulating others.

Joyfully receiving the gift of children is the attitude God desires us to have as we think about what it means to be a family. We remember that having children fulfills God's design for marriage and sexuality. Having children brings joy. In fact, a 2007 survey of parents indicated that children (along with one's spouse) rank at the top of the list of things that are a source of adult happiness and fulfillment. Jobs, money, and things can fade away, but having a family can bring people contentment. Once people become parents, they realize what a blessing and joy children can be! That's how God planned it!

How can a woman tell if she's pregnant?

Doctors look for an increase in the size of the uterus and the breasts. The cervix may be softer and may have a bluish tint. They also test the blood or the urine for a hormonal change that can be detected about ten days after conception.

A woman may notice any or all of the following symptoms: a missed period, breast fullness and tenderness, prebreakfast nausea, unusual tiredness, frequency of urination. However, all these symptoms may have other causes. It is possible (but unusual) for a pregnant woman to have a normal period.

While home pregnancy tests are readily available today, their accuracy rate is not 100 percent. Since early diagnosis of pregnancy is very important, it is far better to see a physician. There are many substances—medicines, cigarette smoke, alcohol, drugs—that can severely damage the developing baby. Pregnant mothers who are in good physical condition have much healthier babies and are less likely to have problems during pregnancy and **delivery**.

What happens after the egg and the sperm meet in the fallopian tube?

The fertilized egg fastens itself to the cushiony wall of the uterus. A thin, tough bag called the **amnion** forms around the egg. It is filled with a watery liquid called **amniotic fluid**. The developing baby (called an embryo at this stage) floats in the liquid, which protects it from bumps or changes in temperature. Waste materials go into the amniotic fluid.

At the end of two months, the embryo has a brain, a heart, a liver, eyes, ears, arms, and legs—not fully developed yet, but recognizable. After the eighth week, the human embryo is called a human fetus. By this time, a flat network of blood vessels, the **placenta**, has formed on the uterus wall. Mother and baby have separate bloodstreams. The placenta is close to the mother's blood vessels so that food and oxygen can filter through it to the **umbilical cord** and on to the fetus.

During the third and fourth months, nails begin to form on fingers and toes. Sex organs develop. The mother has the thrilling experience of feeling a little flutter inside her as the baby moves. As the fetus continues to grow, the mother's uterus and abdomen stretch to many times their original size. She becomes more conscious of the baby moving inside her.

How is the baby's sex decided?

All human cells, including sperm and egg cells, have twenty-three pairs of **chromosomes**. The chromosomes each contain many **genes**, different characteristics that are passed on to the next generation. About half of a man's sperm cells have a male chromosome; the other half have a female chromosome. The question of whether the baby will be a boy or a girl depends on which sperm happens to reach the egg cell first.

Most pregnant women have a checkup about once a month to see how the baby is growing. With a special ultrasound machine, doctors can see how the baby is developing in the uterus. The image seen on the machine is called a sonogram. The doctor or technician can take a picture to show the baby to the family. The sonogram can also show whether the baby is a boy or a girl.

What decides color of hair, musical ability, intelligence—all the things people inherit from their parents?

People inherit possibilities from their parents—possibilities that they may or may not develop in life. These possibilities may include athletic, intellectual, and musical abilities. Most of us inherit far more natural talent than we ever use. However, all these possibilities are in the new cell that forms when the sperm meets the egg. A woman's body makes hundreds of egg cells in her lifetime, each with a different combination of genes. Some genes carry characteristics she does not have herself, such as red hair like her great-grandfather's.

A man's body makes billions of sperm cells in his lifetime, each with a different combination of genes from his family. During intercourse, an average man may release 50 million sperm cells when he ejaculates. The baby's characteristics will depend on which sperm cell meets which egg cell. One of the special wonders of parenthood is seeing some of your own characteristics blended with those of the person you love, creating a totally unique individual.

What happens in childbirth?

During **labor**, powerful muscles in the uterus contract for thirty seconds or so, then relax. At first, the contractions feel like mild menstrual cramps and are about fifteen to twenty minutes apart, but gradually they become stronger and closer together. The uterus is slowly pushing the baby downward. At some point, the bag of amniotic fluid breaks and the liquid flows out through the vagina.

Gradually the cervix opening expands from about 1/8 inch to about 4 inches. More contractions push the baby down into the vagina. The mother contracts her abdominal muscles to push; often, the father helps by holding her and encouraging her. Many parents-to-be attend classes that prepare them for this moment.

The baby's head usually appears first, then one shoulder followed by the other. The doctor guides and supports—but never pulls—the baby until it is born.

When the baby is breathing normally, the umbilical cord is cut about three inches from the abdomen. In time, the stump will dry and fall off, leaving a navel behind.

The placenta is no longer needed to nourish the baby and is now expelled from the mother's body. The entire birth process, from first labor pains until delivery, ordinarily takes eight to twenty hours for a first child.

In some situations, mothers have a **Cesarean birth** (also known as a C-section), in which the mother has surgery. The baby is delivered through a surgical cut the doctor makes in the mother's abdomen and uterus. This is more common if the mother is thirty-five years old or older or if the baby is in a **breech** position (where the baby has not turned into a head-down position but is feet-first).

Most babies are born in hospitals, but it is possible for a mother to give birth to a healthy baby at home or at a birthing center. Doctors and nurses help make the mother and baby more comfortable. The baby's father often helps too. More and more women are getting help and support from a trained caregiver such as a midwife or doula, a specially trained person who helps women and their families before, during, and after labor.

Is childbirth painful?

As a result of the fall into sin, women experience pain during childbirth. The muscles of the uterus, which have stretched to make room for the growing baby, tighten and push, forcing the baby from the uterus into the vagina. This process can take many hours. Many hospitals and other agencies offer childbirth classes, sometimes called Lamaze classes, which teach both mother and father what to expect during labor and delivery. In the months before their baby's birth, both parents can attend these classes to become familiar with the process and to learn exercises and breathing techniques that will give the mother some control over the pain. Pregnant women who are well informed about what to expect tend to be more relaxed and therefore experience less pain. Many women learn exercises and breathing techniques that give them some control over the process. Each individual is different, though. Some women choose to take medication to help them control the pain during labor.

Is it harder to give birth to twins or triplets?

Not really. Because she is carrying more weight, the mother may be a little more uncomfortable during the last month or so of pregnancy. Like a single-birth **delivery**, the babies are born one at a time. Since they are likely to be smaller than other babies, they may need special care for a while.

What is the difference between identical twins and fraternal twins?

Fraternal twins are conceived when two different sperm cells join two different egg cells. Although these children often feel especially close to each other, they each inherited a different set of characteristics from their parents.

Identical twins are conceived when one sperm cell joins one egg cell and the fertilized cell then splits into two cells. These cells are exactly alike, and each of these divided cells grows into a separate individual. Although identical twins begin life with the same set of inherited characteristics, they have different experiences and make different choices. Each becomes a unique individual, exactly like no one else in the world. Each has his or her own special relationship with God.

If children are a gift from God, why are so many new parents tired and depressed?

All new parents get tired, since it seems the new member of the family is apt to sleep all day and be awake all night. In reality, the newborn baby sleeps and wakes in segments a few hours each. Caring for a new baby is a lot of work, especially during the first month or two.

Normal hormonal changes in a new mother's body also can cause sadness. With the support of her husband, other family members, and friends, mothers usually get past this period of sadness. For others, the depression can be more severe. About 11 percent of women are diagnosed with the more serious postpartum depression. It is best for the mother to work with a counselor or psychiatrist to help her through this type of depression.

New parents can become upset because they don't measure up to their own ideals of what a good parent should be and do. They can't always soothe the baby when he or she is crying. Perhaps the mother is unable to nurse the baby as she had hoped. There is much that new parents get anxious about. It is good to have family or friends to help calm the new parents' anxieties and to pray continually to God for patience, wisdom, and understanding. It is never too early to take children to worship, to read them Bible stories, and to talk to them about faith in Christ. This alone brings much comfort to anxious parents.

Sometimes new parents need professional guidance as they struggle to adjust. They may seek out prayer and counsel from a pastor, their own parents, or older friends who have already experienced similar struggles. If parents continue to have difficulties adjusting to the demands of being a parent, they may benefit from the services of a trained Christian counselor who can help them.

Of course, although parents love their baby, almost any parent may sometimes feel like he or she doesn't *like* their baby very much, or at least they may feel frustrated with the challenges of parenting. They may resent the changes the baby has brought to their lives; they may feel trapped, weighed down by responsibility. Adding a third person (or more) to a family changes the whole family dynamics (e.g., the time husband and wife can spend together, finances, etc.). Communication between husband and wife is vitally important as caretaking roles are shared and as both parents lovingly, unselfishly care for the baby and for each other.

When they give each other love, understanding, and support, this shared experience will end up being a very positive one. Talking about feelings helps, as does prayer and leaning on the strength God gives through His Word.

As time goes on, the new parents will find that, although feelings of irritation and anger come and go, their love for their child is a basic, ongoing, growing part of their love for each other and for God. They won't be able to imagine their lives without their child—and they wouldn't want it any other way! Sure, children are a responsibility, but they are such a blessing (Psalm 127:3–4). For all the challenging times, there are many more moments that are rewarding, delightful, and filled with joy.

What is a miscarriage?

Sometimes a fetus does not develop properly, so the uterus pushes it out of the body. This is called a **miscarriage** and is most likely to happen during the first seven weeks of pregnancy. Natural miscarriages happen to many women, and many of them may not even know they are pregnant when it happens. It is estimated that around half of all fertilized eggs die and are lost spontaneously. For those who are already aware of the child growing inside them (15–20 percent of pregnancies), a miscarriage can bring deep heartache and sadness. However, many healthy women do go on to have babies even after they have suffered a miscarriage.

What is a premature baby?

Approximately 13 percent of babies are born before thirty-seven weeks of pregnancy, which is **premature**, or early; full-term is forty weeks (nine months). Since 1980, the premature birth rate has increased by 36 percent.

If a baby is born more than a month early, she or he will probably weigh less than 6 pounds. Babies that small may need special care to survive, but those born at twenty-seven weeks have a 90 percent chance of survival. A baby weighing less than 2 pounds has only a small chance of survival, although new medical techniques now make it possible for doctors to save very tiny babies. Babies have been known to live if they were born at twenty-two or twenty-three weeks. Babies who have not been born yet are still living people. It is God's design that babies fully develop inside their mother's uterus for forty weeks, but He has blessed us with many medical advances that help babies who are born prematurely.

What causes birth defects?

About 2.5 percent of babies are born with a birth defect of some kind. Some defects are inherited; others are caused by outside factors such as drugs, infection, STDs, alcohol, smoking, poor nutrition, radiation, or pollutants. The risks are greater for pregnant women younger than eighteen or older than thirty-five. Early diagnosis of pregnancy is important because commonly prescribed medicines may be harmful to a developing baby. Even a father's exposure to some chemicals can cause birth defects in babies conceived while the chemical remains in the father's body.

Women who have what is called Rh-negative blood cells also risk birth defects in their second pregnancy. If the baby has Rh-positive blood, the mother's body will attack the baby's red blood cells. This can be prevented by vaccination after the birth of a first baby or after a miscarriage.

Everyone should have a complete physical examination before marriage. For women, the exam should include blood tests to check immunity to rubella and to find out blood type. Babies born to mothers who have rubella (German measles) during pregnancy often have serious birth defects. Doctors recommend that females be vaccinated against rubella while they are young girls, long before they conceive a child. A woman should not become pregnant until at least three months after vaccination.

Why are some couples unable to have a child?

Infertility means not being able to get pregnant after one year of trying. Infertility can occur if there are problems with any of the many things that have to happen to result in pregnancy (e.g., **ovulation**, fertilization, implantation). The top causes of infertility are problems with the female's fallopian tubes or the male's sperm. For those who are sexually active without protection, there is a 90 percent chance that a pregnancy will happen within a year, but for those who want a child and can't conceive, there can be much sadness. As Christians, we have an opportunity to pray for those experiencing heartache. Jesus is with us always and sustains us through His Word during difficult times.

In many cases, the causes of infertility are unknown. Some people delay childbearing until their thirties or forties, and their chances of conceiving a child decrease as they grow older. Some diseases and infections can damage the reproductive organs. However, couples who fail to conceive within the first two years of unprotected intercourse have a better chance than ever before of achieving conception with medical help. If they seek treatment, many will succeed in conceiving. Of those treated for infertility, 67 percent will go on to have a baby.

Should married couples use birth control to avoid conceiving children?

Considering the command and blessing of God to Adam and Eve to have children, couples today should enter marriage with the intent to welcome any children God may give them. For Christian couples, the decision to intentionally avoid conceiving a child should be made with great thought and prayerful consideration. The married couple must seriously consider *why* they want to avoid children and if such motives are God-pleasing.

In the event of a need for such a difficult decision, there are a variety of contraceptives available for couples to use today, ranging from condoms, to birth control pills and patches, to barrier products such as a diaphragm, to **natural family planning**. These methods have varying levels of effectiveness, but none is 100 percent effective. When using hormonal or chemical contraceptives, it is important to verify that such pills do not destroy already-fertilized eggs or create a hostile womb that would cause a fertilized egg to perish. Such methods destroy human life, which is disobedient to God's will and does not honor the life He created.

- IUDs (or intrauterine devices) are small, T-shaped devices placed inside the uterus by a doctor. Depending on the type, they stay in the uterus for five to ten years.

- Birth control pills taken regularly by a woman prevent ovulation by making the body "think" it is pregnant. Nonetheless, approximately one out of eleven women currently using the birth control pill will become pregnant within a year.

- An implant is a thin rod that is inserted under the skin of a woman's upper arm. Over three years, a hormone that prevents pregnancy continues to be released.

- A birth control shot can be given every three months. Approximately one out of seventeen women currently getting the shot will become pregnant within a year.

- A birth control patch can be worn on the skin. A new one is placed each week, except the fourth week so the woman can have her period. Approximately one out of eleven women currently wearing a patch will become pregnant within a year.

- A birth control ring can be placed inside the vagina for three weeks and then removed the fourth week so the woman can have her period. Approximately one out of eleven women currently wearing a ring will become pregnant within a year.

- **Spermicides** are foams, gels, creams, or tablets that are placed inside the vagina before sex to kill sperm. One in three or four women currently using spermicides will become pregnant within a year.

- A contraceptive sponge is a doughnut-shaped barrier placed into the vagina before sex to kill sperm and keep them from reaching the egg. Almost one out of four women currently using the sponge will become pregnant within a year.

- The diaphragm is a cap that a woman inserts into her vagina before sex to keep the sperm from getting into her uterus.

- Condoms fit over the penis and prevent the sperm from entering the vagina. Approximately one out of six women whose partner currently uses a condom will become pregnant within a year. There is also a female condom. Approximately one out of five women currently using a female condom will become pregnant within a year. Condoms are the only form of birth control that will help protect against some—but not all—sexually transmitted diseases (STDs).

- In the Natural Family Planning (NFP) method, a woman closely keeps track of her monthly periods and ovulation cycles, avoiding intercourse during those times each month when she is most likely to be fertile and get pregnant. This can be used with other methods of birth control to increase their effectiveness. A woman who is using only NFP has a one-in-four chance of becoming pregnant.

- Men and women also can be sterilized by having an operation that prevents pregnancy. On the man, this is done by cutting the tubes that carry sperm from the testicles. The procedure is called a **vasectomy**. On the woman, it's done by blocking, cutting, or tying shut the fallopian tubes. This is called **tubal ligation**. Women can also have a **hysterectomy**, in which all or part of the uterus is removed. All of these **sterilization** operations are usually permanent. They do not, however, affect the ability to have sexual intercourse.

Many Christians are concerned about the motives for practicing birth control, particularly if the couple does not want children and the responsibilities that children bring. God did institute marriage for the procreation of children (Genesis 1:28). Some Christian churches permit only "natural methods" of birth control since they view other methods as being against God's will. They feel God determines when or if couples should have a child. Another major concern for Christians is that some contraceptives can aggressively attack the sperm and egg *after* fertilization—after a life has been created—in effect, causing an abortion or making the uterus too hostile for a baby to survive.

A married couple must spend time in prayer to God and conversation with each other to best understand why they would choose to use birth control to prevent pregnancy. Our Lord urges us to trust in Him for all our needs, and this certainly extends to God supplying what we need physically and emotionally to have and care for a child.

But aren't there too many people in the world already? I hear about overpopulation on the news and worry that humans are causing a lot of problems for the planet.

The truth is that many nations are facing a crisis precisely because they are not having enough children. Many men and women so highly value their independence that they do not want the responsibility of taking care of children. European women are having so few children that many European countries are unable to sustain even a basic replacement rate of 2.1 children per woman. Even the United States has fallen below replacement level (1.9 children per woman in 2010).

A replacement rate is related to the number of deaths per births. It is the number of children each woman needs to have to maintain current population levels (or zero population growth). What this means is that there won't be enough workers to fill all the jobs, and there will be more people receiving Social Security than those who can pay into the system, among many other concerns.

It is a serious danger to build society around principles that contradict God's plan for humans. In this case, the idea that children are not to be valued and lovingly welcomed into every home because they might be an "inconvenience" is a growing concern.

Shouldn't I learn more about birth control now in case I find myself in a situation where I need it?

Our culture works hard to convince young people to learn about birth control so they can have "**safe sex**." God has a different idea. He teaches us that we are all part of His divine plan for loving, intimate communion within the boundaries of marriage. He also teaches us that we can train ourselves to respect and care for others with the same self-giving love He extends to us. We all have a choice to make daily—whether we will receive and embrace the gifts God gives us or reject these gifts and try to carve out a life apart from Him.

The variety and availability of birth control methods reflect a shift in our society's attitudes toward children, viewing them as projects to be planned or products that are made when we choose to make them. Birth control methods are readily available and to a certain extent remove the fear of pregnancy, perhaps encouraging or condoning unmarried couples to engage in premarital sex. Certainly this is not how God designed the gift of marriage and sexuality.

Conclusion

There you have it! The answer to all your questions. Well, maybe not *all* of them. As you grow as a Christian into adulthood, you will have many more questions. Talking to a parent or another Christian man you respect and trust is vital to helping you navigate these tough waters.

It is not easy being a Christian man in today's world. Actually, we know from the Bible that it has never been easy to be a man of God. We do know that God remains faithful and, through His Spirit, helps us grow and mature into adult Christians. The Bible completely reveals the story of your salvation in Christ. It reveals God's design and plan for His people. God reveals the marvels of His creation and your unique design as man.

Pray that God will bless you with a wife. Pray also for the strength to remain sexually pure until that blessing comes. Even if you are not blessed with the gift of a wife, know that God's plan for you is not all that different if you remain single: He wants you to love and serve your neighbor.

"For you were called to freedom, brothers. Only do not use your freedom as an opportunity for the flesh, but through love serve one another" (Galatians 5:13).

Grow and be confident in the Lord from this day forward!

Sexually Transmitted Diseases (STDs)

The most serious STDs are **HIV/AIDS, gonorrhea, syphilis, genital herpes, chlamydia, trichomoniasis**, and **human papillomavirus (HPV)**. Although a yeast infection can be passed on by sexual contact, it is not considered an STD because it has many other possible causes.

Why are STDs dangerous?

People may have an STD without realizing it.

Infected people are misled when symptoms disappear temporarily. However, the symptoms usually come back worse than before.

Some consequences of untreated STDs are blindness, arthritis, mental illness, **sterility**, cancer, or death.

Babies born from an infected mother may have major birth defects.

How does a person get an STD?

The bacteria, viruses, or parasites that cause STDs live on the warm, damp surfaces of the body. The diseases are most often spread by intercourse or intimate sexual activity in which these surfaces touch each other.

Because the HIV/AIDS virus also lives in blood, HIV can be spread through contaminated needles used while injecting illegal drugs into the body. In the 1980s, a few people caught HIV through blood transfusions. Today's testing methods make it almost impossible to get HIV in this way. HIV/AIDS cannot be passed on by ordinary social contact such as handshakes or hugs.

Babies can be born with HIV/AIDS, syphilis, or genital herpes. Syphilis can be caught by kissing a person who has contagious mouth sores. Gonorrhea can be caught by touching infected sexual organs if one's hand has a break in the skin. Trichomoniasis can be passed on by moist towels, bathing suits, or a damp toilet seat. In all these cases, the infected person may not ever realize that he or she has an STD and can pass it on to others.

How can I tell if someone has an STD?

You can't. Only medical tests performed by a doctor can make this diagnosis. A person with a contagious case of an STD may appear perfectly healthy. On the other hand, the symptoms described in the section on STD specifics have many other possible causes. You could do someone a great injustice if you assume that his or her illness is caused by an STD.

STD Specifics

HIV/AIDS

What are the symptoms?
(All people may not notice all symptoms.)

Most people have no early symptoms. The human immunodeficiency virus (HIV) that causes acquired immune deficiency syndrome (AIDS) attacks a person's immune system and damages his or her ability to fight disease. Without a functioning immune system, the person becomes vulnerable to many life-threatening illnesses, such as meningitis, pneumonia, dementia, and cancer. Symptoms of these "opportunistic" diseases include persistent cough and fever associated with shortness of breath or difficulty in breathing and multiple purplish blotches and bumps on the skin. Early symptoms may include thrush (yeast infection on the tongue), vaginal yeast infection or pelvic inflammatory disease, shingles, fever, diarrhea, weight loss, tiredness, and swollen lymph glands.

How soon do the first symptoms appear?

Symptoms may begin in a few weeks or it may take 10 years or more for symptoms to appear.

What happens if the disease is not treated?

There is no known cure for AIDS. Most people who carry the HIV virus look and feel healthy, since it may take as long as 10 years before a person with HIV develops AIDS. Although medical science can prolong the lives of persons with AIDS, AIDS is almost always fatal.

How common is HIV/AIDS?

More than 1.2 million people are infected in the United States, and approximately 50,000 new people are infected each year. Most of the new cases are overwhelmingly among men who have sex with men (MSM). It is expected that the number of people living with HIV will continue to increase because of the life-prolonging HIV treatments available. However, this means that opportunities for transmission also increase. In 2006, it was estimated that there was 1 transmission for every 20 individuals living with HIV.

Gonorrhea

What are the symptoms?
(All people may not notice all symptoms.)

Pain or itching when urinating; frequent, urgent need to urinate; white or yellow discharge from penis or vagina; sore penis or vulva; sore throat.

Most women and some men have no early symptoms. Their only hope is that their sex partners will tell them they may have been infected.

How soon do the first symptoms appear?

Symptoms may appear 2–5 days after exposure, although it could take as long as 30 days. Early symptoms last about 2–3 weeks.

What happens if the disease is not treated?

Men: The germs spread through the body. If untreated, gonorrhea can cause any or all of these problems: abscess in prostate gland; swollen, painful testicles; sterility; kidney damage. It also increases the risk of bladder cancer.

Women: The infection usually centers in the cervix, spreading to all other sexual organs, and may cause painful abscesses that leave scar tissue. The scar tissue often blocks fallopian tubes, making pregnancy impossible or very dangerous. Women can also develop pelvic inflammatory disease (PID).

Both men and women may develop acute arthritis and eye infections.

How common is gonorrhea?

Gonorrhea is a very common sexually transmitted disease. More than 820,000 people are infected each year.

Syphilis

What are the symptoms?
(All people may not notice all symptoms.)

STAGE 1: A sore (usually painless) on the penis, vulva, around the **rectum**, in the mouth, or on the lips. The sore is at the spot where the infection entered the body.

STAGE 2: A rash (sometimes very faint) that may turn into sores in warm, wet areas; temporary hair loss; swollen glands.

How soon do the first symptoms appear?

STAGE 1: The sore may appear 10–90 days or more after exposure. If left alone, the sore will go away within 3–6 weeks, but the disease will remain if untreated.

STAGE 2: Three weeks to 3 months after the sore goes away. Without treatment, these symptoms go away within a few weeks or months. The disease, however, will remain unless treated.

What happens if the disease is not treated?

Syphilis can remain hidden for months or years, even 10–30 years. Only a blood test can detect it. After anywhere from 2 to 40 years, the following symptoms may occur: large destructive sores; heart problems; blindness; numbness or paralysis; dementia or insanity; irreparable damage to a baby during pregnancy; even death.

How common is syphilis?

Roughly 55,400 cases of syphilis were reported in 2013.

Chlamydia

What are the symptoms?
(All people may not notice all symptoms.)

Chlamydia is the most commonly reported STD. Approximately 75 percent of women and 50 percent of men with chlamydia have no early symptoms. Symptoms, when they appear, are similar to those of gonorrhea (see above). Men can have a discharge and a burning while urinating. Women can have an abnormal discharge and a burning sensation when urinating.

Chlamydia bacteria can live in the body for years without causing noticeable symptoms. Faithful married couples are often shocked to learn that they both have chlamydia, caused by a sexual episode in one partner's past.

How soon do the first symptoms appear?

Usually 3 weeks after infection. Most people don't experience any symptoms.

What happens if the disease is not treated?

Men: Inflamed urethra and testicles; possible inflammation of rectum; chronic pelvic pain; if untreated, sterility.

Women: Infected urethra and cervix. It may cause infertility, ectopic pregnancy (pregnancy in the fallopian tube), inflammation of the pelvis, or chronic pelvic pain. It can infect newborn babies. Up to 40 percent of women with untreated chlamydia will develop PID, and 1 in 5 women with PID becomes infertile.

How common is chlamydia?

Nearly 3 million people are infected in the United States each year.

Genital Herpes

What are the symptoms?
(All people may not notice all symptoms.)

Blisters or small bumps on penis and urethra or cervix, vagina, and vulva that may break and form open, painful sores. Often the blisters are so small the person does not realize he or she has the disease and may unknowingly pass it on to others. Many mistake the symptom for a pimple or ingrown hair. There may be pain when urinating. With the first infection, there may also be fever, joint pain, flu-like symptoms, itching, and tingling. Eighty-one percent of people infected are never aware of their condition.

How soon do the first symptoms appear?

Symptoms appear 2–20 days after exposure. They may go away and reappear months later, even if there has been no sexual contact in the meantime. Repeat outbreaks are common.

What happens if the disease is not treated?

The infection may cause birth defects or death for a baby whose mother has herpes. There is strong evidence of a link between genital herpes and cancer of the cervix. Yearly Pap tests are advisable for women.

How common is genital herpes?

Sixteen percent of people ages 14–49—about 1 in 6—have had a genital herpes infection. There are 24 million cases of HSV-1 and 776,000 new cases of HSV-2 in a year.

Human Papillomavirus (HPV; "Genital Warts")

What are the symptoms?
(All people may not notice all symptoms.)

Symptoms include warts on the genital organs, from the size of a small tick to the size of a cauliflower.

How soon do the first symptoms appear?

It may take a few weeks, or years, before HPV symptoms appear.

What happens if the disease is not treated?

The HPV virus may cause cancers of the **anus**, throat, cervix, vagina, vulva, and penis. Ten thousand women in the United States get cervical cancer each year.

How common is HPV?

The Centers for Disease Control and Prevention (CDC) reports that 14 million Americans are infected with HPV each year and the total number of people infected is over 79 million. It is estimated that nearly all sexually active people *outside of marriage* will be infected with HPV at some point in their lives. A vaccine is available to help prevent the spread of HPV, and it's not wrong for Christians to have the vaccine, but for Christians, abstinence from sex outside of marriage is the God-pleasing method of prevention.

Trichomoniasis

What are the symptoms?
(All people may not notice all symptoms.)

Women: Clear, white, or yellowish-green discharge with a strong odor; pain in pelvic area; soreness or severe itching in vulva.

Men: Most have no symptoms, but some will experience a thin, whitish discharge, especially in the morning or a tingling, itching sensation in the penis.

How soon do the first symptoms appear?

They appear 5–28 days after exposure. Symptoms come and go.

What happens if the disease is not treated?

The tiny parasites that cause "trich" will probably continue to multiply and cause discomfort. There is a link between trichomoniasis and cervical cancer. There is an increased risk of getting or spreading other STDs.

Infected women are more likely to have a preterm delivery and a child with low birth weight.

How common is trichomoniasis?

More than 3.7 million people in the U.S. have trichomoniasis. Over 1 million new cases occur each year. Although it is most commonly spread by sexual contact, you can also be infected through contact with damp or moist objects such as towels, wet clothing, and toilet seats.

Other Questions

How can a person tell if he has an STD?

An examination by a doctor is the only way to find out for sure. If you notice any symptoms, see a doctor as soon as possible. An STD is easier to stop if it is diagnosed early and correctly. Do not try to treat yourself with antibiotics or other medicines. Each disease requires a different treatment. In some cases, the disease can be cured; some others cannot be cured, although treatment may be available to treat the symptoms.

There are other possible causes for most of the symptoms. For instance, pain during urination may be caused by a kidney or bladder infection. A discharge from the vagina could be perfectly normal or it could be a yeast infection (not an STD). If you are in doubt, see a doctor. Knowing for sure that you do not have an STD is important for your peace of mind.

Clearly, the best approach is to avoid contracting STDs in the first place. For Christians, abstinence from sex outside of marriage is the God-pleasing method of prevention. A husband and wife who remained sexually pure before marriage are sure to share a life free from STDs.

Are you immune to an STD after you have had it?

No. The same person can get it again and again.

How likely am I to get an STD?

Remaining sexually pure, as God designed, certainly is the best prevention. However, it's important to inform yourself about STDs because

- you may need to advise and counsel friends who are less informed;

- it is possible—though unlikely—for a person who is not sexually active to get an STD; and

- an untreated STD could destroy not only your life, but the lives of your spouse and your baby.

Where can I go for help?

Here are some possibilities:

- Your parents. Most parents are loving, supportive, and forgiving when their teenagers come to them with major problems.

- Your family doctor. Be honest with your doctor. Without information only you can give, he or she may not test for an STD as the possible cause of your symptoms.

- A trusted school nurse or school counselor. They will know where you can go for diagnosis and treatment.

- Your pastor, a teacher, youth counselor, or some other trusted adult at your church. Caring about your physical and spiritual health, this individual can guide and help you.

- Your local public health clinic. Look under your city or county name in the phone book. A public clinic is sometimes crowded and impersonal, but you are likely to find caring and competent people there. Public health doctors see so many STD cases that they become experts in their treatment. There will probably be no charge. If you are a minor, be sure to seek your parents' advice and help before taking action.

Glossary

Abortion (a-BOR-shun) The premature termination of a pregnancy.

There are three types:

Voluntary   A procedure performed at the request of the pregnant woman.

Spontaneous ("miscarriage") A natural termination usually due to some abnormal development of the fetus.

Therapeutic   A medically recommended procedure prompted by abnormal developments that threaten the life of the mother.

Some common methods of induced abortion:

Aspiration ("suction aspiration," "suction curettage," "vacuum aspiration") A medical procedure in which the cervix is dilated and a long plastic tube connected to a suction device is inserted into the uterus to suction out the fetus and placenta. Used during weeks 6–16 of pregnancy.

D&E ("dilation and extraction") A medical procedure performed after 21 weeks gestation in which the cervix is dilated and the fetus extracted.

Medical abortion Most common method of abortion, using prescription mifepristone and misoprostol (also known as "RU-486") in combination, causes embryos to detach from the uterine wall. The woman must be no more than 7 weeks pregnant, with medical care nearby in case of complications.

Menstrual extraction ("regulation") Extracting the lining of the uterus (normally part of the menstrual process) by a suction technique; normally done within two weeks after a missed menstrual period, before positive diagnosis of pregnancy can be made.

Morning-after pill Prescription drug taken by the woman in a single dosage after sexual intercourse to prevent fertilization of the egg or to prevent implantation of an already fertilized egg. This later use is why this drug is considered an *abortifacient* (to cause an abortion).

133

RU-486 (Also known by medication names "mifepristone and misoprostol") Prescription medicine taken by the woman to detach the embryo from the uterus. Like the morning-after pill, abortifacient RU-486 does not prevent conception. When taken shortly after the first missed menstrual period, RU-486 causes the newly attached embryo to detach from the lining of the uterus and subsequently to slough off with the menstrual flow.

Saline abortion A saline (salt) solution is injected into the woman's uterus, causing abortion to occur. Used only after fourteenth week of pregnancy. This procedure is only rarely done in the United States (less than 1 percent of abortions).

Vacuum curettage After dilation of the cervix, suction is used to empty the uterus. Can be used up to the twelfth week of pregnancy.

Abstinence (AB-stin-ens) Voluntarily avoiding something. In sexual connotation, refraining from sexual activity.

Adolescence (ad-uh-LES-sens) The period of life between puberty and adulthood.

Adultery (a-DULL-ter-ee) Sexual intercourse with a person who is legally married to someone else. The term is often used to describe any sexual intercourse outside of marriage.

AIDS Acquired Immune Deficiency Syndrome. A life-threatening viral disease most commonly transmitted through blood or semen or both, either by sexual contact or by use of dirty needles when "shooting" drugs.

Amnion (AM-nee-on) The thin membrane that forms the sac surrounding the fetus within the uterus. Contains amniotic fluid in which the fetus is immersed for protection against shocks and jolts.

Androgen (AN-dro-jen) A hormone that influences growth and the sex drive in the male. Produces masculine secondary sex characteristics (voice changes, hair growth, etc.).

Androgynous (an-DROJ-e-ness) Genderless, neither having specifically masculine or feminine characteristics.

Anus (AY-nuss) The opening at the base of the buttocks through which solid waste is eliminated from the intestines.

Artificial insemination The medical procedure of injecting semen into the vagina close to the cervix by artificial means; can enable pregnancy in spite of fertility problems.

Birth control See *Contraception*.

Bisexual   (by-SECKS-shoo-al) A person who has sexual attraction to both sexes.

Bladder   (BLAD-er) A sac in the pelvic region where urine is stored until elimination.

Breech   The birth position when the baby's feet or buttocks appear first in the birth canal instead of his or her head.

Celibate   (SELL-ih-bet) Abstaining from sexual intercourse

Cervix   (SER-viks) The narrow, lower part of the uterus, which opens into the deep portion of the vagina.

Cesarean   (si-SAIR-ee-an) **birth** ("Cesarean section"; "C-section") Delivery of a baby by surgical incision through the abdomen into the uterus.

Chancre   (SHANG-ker) A small sore or ulcerated area, usually on the genitals, which can be an early symptom of syphilis.

Chastity   (CHAS-ti-tee) Cultivating a life of purity whether single or married.

Chlamydia (kla-MID-ee-ah) See *Sexually transmitted disease.*

Chromosome (KRO-mo-soam) One of the more or less rodlike bodies found in the nucleus of all cells, containing the heredity factors or genes. Twenty-two pairs of chromosomes account for a person's hereditary characteristics. The 23rd pair determines sex. See *X chromosome* and *Y chromosome*.

Cilia   (SIL-ee-uh) (plural of *cilium*) Tiny hairlike processes often forming part of a fringe, especially on a cell, capable of lashing movement—tiny eyelash-like hairs moving something forward.

Circumcision (ser-kum-SIZH-un) Surgical removal of the foreskin or prepuce of the penis. Originally a Jewish rite performed as a sign of reception into their faith; now generally performed for purposes of cleanliness.

Climax   See *Orgasm*.

Clitoris   (KLIT-or-is) A small, highly sensitive female sex organ located just above the urethra.

Coitus   (KOI-tus) ("copulation") Sexual intercourse between male and female, in which the penis is inserted into the vagina.

Conception (kon-SEP-shun) ("impregnation") Penetration of the ovum (female egg cell) by a sperm, resulting in development of an embryo—new life.

Condom See *Contraception.*

Contraception (kon-trah-SEP-shun) ("birth control") The prevention of conception by use of devices, drugs, or other means in sexual intercourse.

Cowper's glands Small glands lying alongside the male urethra that secrete part of the seminal fluid.

Cunnilingus (kun-i-LING-us) The act of applying the mouth or tongue to the vulva to stimulate the female.

Delivery The process of giving birth.

Douching (DOOSH-ing) The cleansing of the vagina with a stream of liquid solution or water.

Ejaculation (ee-jack-yoo-LAY-shun) The discharge of semen from the penis.

Embryo (EM-bree-oh) The unborn in its earliest stages of development. In humans, the fertilized ovum during the first 8 weeks of its growth.

Epididymis (ep-ah-DID-i-miss) The mass of tiny coils connecting the testicles with the sperm duct.

Erection (ee-RECK-shun) The enlargement and hardening of the penis as tissues fill with blood, usually during sexual excitement.

Erogenous (i-RAH-jen-us) **zone** Any area of the body that is sexually sensitive or stimulating such as mouth, lips, breasts, nipples, and genitals.

Erotic (ee-RAH-tik) Sexually stimulating.

Estrogen (ESS-tro-jen) A hormone that affects functioning of the menstrual cycle and produces female secondary sex characteristics (breast development, widened hips, etc.).

Exhibitionist (ex-i-BISH-un-ist) A person who compulsively exposes his or her sex organs publicly or anonymously.

Extramarital (ex-tra-MARE-i-tal) "Outside of marriage"; often used to refer to illicit sexual intercourse, e.g., "extramarital affair."

Fallopian (fa-LOW-pee-an) **tube** The tube through which the egg passes from the ovary to the uterus.

Fellatio (fel-LAY-show) The act of applying the mouth or tongue to the penis to stimulate the male.

Fertility The ability to reproduce.

Fertilization Penetration of the female ovum by a single sperm, resulting in conception.

Fetus (FEE-tuss) The unborn child from the third month after conception until birth.

Follicle (FALL-ick-l) A vesicle in the ovary that contains a developing egg surrounded by a covering of cells. A mature follicle ruptures during ovulation to release an egg.

Foreplay The beginning stage of sexual intercourse, during which partners may kiss, caress, and touch each other in order to achieve full sexual arousal.

Foreskin The loose skin covering the tip of the penis, removed during circumcision. Also called the prepuce (PREE-pus).

Fornication (for-ni-KAY-shun) Sexual intercourse between unmarried men and women.

Genes (jeans) The carriers for hereditary traits in chromosomes.

Genital herpes See *Sexually transmitted disease.*

Genitals (JEN-i-tals) ("genitalia"; "genital organs") Visible reproductive or sex organs. Usually denotes vagina, vulva, and clitoris in females and the penis and testicles in males.

Gestation (jes-TAY-shun) The period from conception to birth, approximately 9 months for humans.

Glans (glanz) The head of the penis exposed when the foreskin is pushed back or after circumcision.

Gonorrhea (gon-er-EE-uh) See *Sexually transmitted disease.*

Gynecologist (guy-na-KOLL-o-jist) A physician who specializes in the treatment of female sexual and reproductive organs.

Heredity (her-ED-it-ee) Relating to that which is transmitted from parents to children, including physical traits, characteristics, or diseases.

Heterosexual (het-er-o-SECK-shoo-al) Relating to sexual attraction to persons of the other sex.

HIV   Human Immunodeficiency Virus; the virus that causes AIDS.

Homosexual (ho-mo-SECK-shoo-al) Relating to sexual attraction to persons of the same sex.

Hormone (HOR-moan) A chemical substance, produced by an endocrine gland, that has a particular effect on the function of other organs in the body.

Human papillomavirus (pap-il-LO-ma-vi-rus) **(HPV)** See *Sexually transmitted disease.*

Hymen   (HIGH-men) A thin membrane that partially closes the entrance to the vagina.

Hysterectomy (hiss-ter-ECK-toh-mee) Surgical removal of the uterus. May include removal of one or both ovaries (oophorectomy).

Impotent (IM-po-tent) Unable to achieve or maintain erection of the penis during sexual intercourse. Impotence is a type of male sexual dysfunction that has many causes.

Incest   (IN-sest) Sexual intercourse between close relatives such as father and daughter, mother and son, or brother and sister; usually a form of sexual abuse.

Infertility (in-fer-TILL-ih-tee) Refers to couples who have not become pregnant after at least one year of unprotected sex.

Intercourse, Sexual See *Coitus.*

Jock itch A fungal infection causing skin irritation in the genital area.

Labor   The birth stage in which the cervix gradually dilates, allowing strong contractions of the uterine muscles to push the baby through the vagina and out of the mother's body.

Lesbian   (LEZ-be-an) A woman who is sexually attracted to other women.

Libido   (li-BEE-doe) See *Sex drive.*

Masturbation (mass-ter-BAY-shun) Self-stimulation of one's sex organs, often to the point of orgasm.

Menarche (MEN-arc-ee) The onset of the menstrual cycle in a girl.

Menopause (MEN-o-pawz) ("change of life"; "climacteric") The end of menstruation in women, usually between the ages 45–55.

Menstruation (men-stroo-AY-shun) The discharge through the vagina of blood and lining from the uterus. This menstrual "period" usually occurs every 28–30 days in females, between puberty and menopause.

Miscarriage The process through which a mother's body expels a baby that died in the womb.

Natural Family Planning See *Contraception*.

Nocturnal emission (nok-TER-nal ee-MISH-un) ("wet dream") Involuntary male erection and ejaculation during sleep.

Obstetrician (ob-ste-TRISH-un) A physician who specializes in the care of women during pregnancy and childbirth, and immediately thereafter.

Oral sex See *Cunnilingus; Fellatio*.

Orgasm (OR-gazm) ("climax") The peak of excitement in sexual activity.

Ovaries (OH-va-rees) The two female sex glands found on either side of the uterus, in which the ova (egg cells) are formed. They also produce hormones that influence female body characteristics.

Ovulation (ah-vyoo-LAY-shun) Release of the mature (ripe) ovum from the ovary to the fallopian tube.

Ovum (OH-vum) (Plural: *ova*) Female reproductive cell (egg) found in the ovary. After fertilization by a male sperm, the human egg develops into an embryo and then a fetus.

Penis (PEE-nis) Male sex organ through which semen is discharged and urine is passed.

Pituitary (pih-TOO-it-air-ee) A gland at the base of the brain that controls functions of all the other ductless glands, especially sex glands, adrenals, and thyroid.

Placenta (pluh-SEN-ta) ("afterbirth") The sponge-like organ that connects the fetus to the lining of the uterus by means of the umbilical cord. It serves to feed the fetus and to dispose of waste. Expelled from the uterus after the birth of a child.

Pornography (por-NOG-raf-ee) Literature, motion pictures, art, or other means of expression that, without any concern for personal or moral values, intend simply to be sexually arousing.

Pregnancy (PREG-nan-see) Period from conception to birth; the condition of having a developing embryo or fetus within the female body.

Premature (PREE-mah-tyoor) When a baby is born too early, before the usual 9 months of growing in the uterus has passed.

Prenatal (pree-NAY-tal) Before birth.

Progesterone (pro-JES-te-roan) The female "pregnancy hormone" that prepares the uterus to receive the fertilized ovum.

Promiscuous (pro-MISS-kyoo-us) Engaging in sexual intercourse with many persons; engaging in casual sexual relationships.

Prostate (PRAH-state) Male gland that surrounds the urethra and neck of the bladder and secretes part of the seminal fluid.

Prostitute (PRAH-sti-toot) An individual who engages in sexual activity for money or other goods.

Puberty (PYOO-ber-tee) The period of rapid development that marks the end of childhood; sex organs mature and produce either eggs or sperm; the girl becomes a young woman and the boy a young man.

Pubic (PYOO-bik) Regarding the lower part of the abdominal area, where hair grows in a triangular patch.

Rape (rayp) Forcible sexual intercourse with a person who does not consent.

Rectum (RECK-tum) The lower end of the large intestine, ending at the anus.

Safe period The interval in the menstrual cycle when the female is presumably not ovulating and therefore unable to become pregnant.

Safe sex The claim that using appropriate "safeguards" such as condoms will keep people from getting pregnant or from getting STDs. The only truly safe sex is to remain a virgin until married and then have intercourse only with an uninfected spouse.

Scrotum (SKRO-tum) The sac of skin suspended between the male's legs that contains the testicles.

Semen (SEE-men) ("seminal fluid"; "seminal emission") The fluid made up of sperm, secretions from the seminal vesicles, prostate and Cowper's glands, and the epididymis. Ejaculated through the penis when the male reaches orgasm.

Seminal vesicles (SEM-i-nal VESS-i-cals) Two storage pouches for sperm (which is produced in the testicles). Located on either side of the prostate, they are attached to and open into the sperm ducts.

Sex drive ("libido") The desire for sexual activity.

Sex organs Commonly refers to the male penis and female vagina.

Sexual dysfunction Term used to describe problems in sexual performance, which could be physical or emotional in nature.

Sexual intercourse See *Coitus.*

Sexually transmitted disease (STD) Any of a variety of contagious diseases contracted almost entirely by sexual intercourse. Some of the most common are AIDS, chlamydia, genital herpes, gonorrhea, human papillomavirus (HPV), trichomoniasis, and syphilis.

Sperm The male reproductive cell(s), produced in the testicles, having the capacity to fertilize the female ova, resulting in pregnancy.

Spermatic duct (sper-MAT-ik dukt) ("Vas deferens") The tube in the male through which sperm passes from the epididymis to the seminal vesicles and urethra.

Spermatic cord The tube in the male by which the testicle is suspended; contains the sperm ducts, veins, and nerves.

Spermicide See *Contraception.*

Sterility (ster-ILL-it-ee) The inability to reproduce.

Sterilization (ster-ill-ih-ZAY-shun) A procedure by which a male or female is rendered unable to produce children but can still engage in sexual intercourse. Some of the most common surgical methods include the following:

    Laparoscopic (la-pa-RO-sko-pic) **sterilization** Tiny incisions in the abdomen, through which the fallopian tubes are cut or cauterized. Also called Band-Aid sterilization.

    Tubal ligation (TOO-bul lie-GAY-shun) The surgeon cuts and ties the ends of both fallopian tubes after making a larger incision in the abdomen or by going through the vagina.

    Vasectomy (vas-ECK-toe-mee) The male sperm-carrying duct is cut, part is removed, and the ends tied.

Syphilis (SIF-i-lis) See *Sexually transmitted disease.*

Testicles (TESS-ti-klz) (Testes) The two male sex glands that produce sperm. They are suspended within a sac of skin between the legs, behind the penis.

Testosterone (tes-TOSS-ter-own) Male sex hormone produced by the testicles; causes and maintains male secondary sex characteristics (voice change, hair growth, etc.).

Transgender (trans-GEN-der) One who feels that their sexual identity does not match the sexual organs with which they were born.

Transvestite One who has a compulsion to dress in the clothing of the other sex.

Trichomoniasis (trick-uh-muh-NY-uh-sis) See *Sexually transmitted disease.*

Tubal ligation See *Sterilization.*

Umbilical cord (um-BILL-i-kal) The cord connecting the fetus to the placenta, through which the fetus receives nourishment.

Urethra (yoo-REE-thra) The duct through which urine passes from the bladder and is eliminated from the body.

Urologist (yoo-RAHL-i-jist) A physician who specializes in treating urinary tract problems of both sexes, as well as the genital tract of males.

Uterus (YOO-ter-us) The small, muscular, pear-shaped female organ in which the fetus develops; has the ability to expand to accommodate the growing child (children).

Vagina (vuh-JY-na) ("birth canal") The canal in the female body between the uterus and the vulva that receives the penis during intercourse; the canal through which an infant passes at birth.

Vas deferens (VAS DEF-er-enz) See *Spermatic duct.*

Vasectomy See *Sterilization.*

Virgin (VER-jin) A person who has never had sexual intercourse.

Vulva (VUL-va) The female's external sex organs, including the labia majora and labia minora, the outer and inner folds of skin (lips) surrounding the vagina, and the clitoris.

Wet dream See *Nocturnal emission.*

Womb (WOOM) See *Uterus.*

X chromosome A chromosome that determines sex, present in all female ova and in one-half of a male's sperm. If the egg is fertilized by a sperm having an X chromosome, a female will be conceived (XX).

Y chromosome A sex-determining chromosome present in one-half of a male's sperm. If an ovum is fertilized by a sperm with a Y chromosome, a male will be conceived (XY).